NEVER OFFER
YOUR COMB
TO A BALD MAN

NEVER OFFER YOUR COMB
TO A BALD MAN

How to Get What You Want
by Giving Others What They Need

ALEXANDER J. BERARDI

NEW WORLD LIBRARY
NOVATO, CALIFORNIA

New World Library
14 Pamaron Way
Novato, California 94949

Copyright © 2001 by Alexander J. Berardi

Cover design by Mary Ann Casler
Text design and typography by Mary Ann Casler

Library of Congress Cataloging-in-Publication Data
Berardi, Alexander J.
Never offer your comb to a bald man : leadership skills for the new century / by Alexander J. Berardi.
p   cm.
Includes index.
ISBN 1-57731-126-4
1. Leadership. 2. Helping behavior. I. Title.
HD57.7 .B469 2001
658.4'092—dc21   00-011657

First Printing, March 2001
ISBN 1-57731-126-4
Printed in Canada on acid-free paper
Distributed to the trade by Publishers Group West

10 9 8 7 6 5 4 3 2 1

I dedicate this book to five very special people.
Each played an essential role in seeing this work through.

I owe undying love and gratitude to my mother
Virginia Catherine LoBoves Berardi, who through her actions
revealed to me the limitless riches one finds in serving others,
and to my mate Diane, who on a sunny September day pledged
to stand by me through thick and thin, and has since endured
far more thin than thick.

I owe the life I am joyously experiencing to
a pot and pan salesman from Yazoo City, Mississippi,
who pulled me from the brink of self-destruction when I was twenty,
to an old ragpicker who inspired me to bring my message to the world,
and to a carpenter who works day and night to mend my broken soul.

I love you all.

CONTENTS

ACKNOWLEDGMENTS

Thanks to Georgia Hughes, "editor extraordinaire" — for lending her vision, talent, brilliance, and a bucket load of patience to this project, and to the rest of the wonderful and special people at New World Library who were forced to endure my insanity yet still managed to produce a fine work of art.

And to my clients, associates, and friends who allowed me to expose some delicate and precious parts of their lives as examples for us all to learn from, and who supported this work by offering their unique insight, wisdom and prayers, especially: Bill Bartmann, Aleila Perry Bundles, Robert Bly, Gloria Bologna, Paul and Clara Breier, Leslie Calvin Brown, Tracy Clark, Jim Cathcart, Kenneth Dolan, Rogers M. Fred III, D.V.M., Rose Ann Huber, Wendy Keller, Thomas Kinkade, Ronald L. Kuby, Esq., Michael LeBoeuf, Ph.D., William Licamele, M.D., Laurie Magers, Joey Novick, Burl V. Pearlmann III, CIW, Wanda Pearlmann, Susan M. Rees, Laura Richie, Henri Roca, M.D., Curtis and Mary Sliwa, Juanell Teague, Hilary H. "Zig" Ziglar, and Patricia A. Zonsa.

And to those who have already passed from this world since this work began: Viktor Frankl, M.D., Don Labruto, Augustine "Og" Mandino, and Judith Lynn Berardi.

And special thanks to my pal Cosmo, who sat patiently by my side through all the writing and swearing.

Okay, fella, we can go for our walk now.

I love you, one and all!

INTRODUCTION

Our beliefs, like the paint-chipped iron bars of a cellblock, can keep us from experiencing the life we have coveted in our dreams. All too often, these beliefs can act as physical reminders of our secret insecurities and self-imposed limitations.

It seems we have accepted the belief that the world is comprised of two mutually exclusive groups of people — those who lead and those who serve. This misconception is as common as an eight-penny nail and just as hard to pry loose from our thoughts and actions. History tells the real truth. The greatest leaders of all time are the *reluctant* ones — those who see their role as one of service — and as an unavoidable consequence of that service were forced to assume the position of leader. The names of those who crave positions of power and authority like a starving dog craves a pound of steak will not be remembered by history. It is instead the quiet ones like Gandhi, Mother Teresa, Jesus, Buddha, Albert Schweitzer, Rosa Parks, who were comfortable serving from the shadows until that inevitable day when they were presented with no other choice but to take the lead and do what needed to be done.

This is a book about those who accepted, albeit reluctantly, the uncommon role of servant leader and as a result took their unique place among the greatest leaders of all time. It is dedicated to and for the benefit of the masses of willing servants who are now or will soon confront the same frightening challenge of leadership.

Servant leaders seem to be derived not from the elitist sources, but rather from the common ranks. For example, Robert Nessen, a practicing New England lawyer, today leads troubled boys away from crime and toward self-reliance by helping them to run their own legitimate business, or Oseola McCarty, a former washerwoman from southern Mississippi, who lived a modest life so that she might one day make it possible for people of color to escape poverty by gaining an education. With a $150,000 contribution to the University of Southern Mississippi that represented her entire life's savings of pennies and quarters, she saw her dream, and the dreams of many deserving and bright young people, become reality.

Servant leaders often hide behind the disguise of people you bump into on the street, and they can also emerge from the least likely candidates of all. Such was the case with Moe Howard — the comical "leader" of the Three Stooges. I met the real Moe Howard nearly twenty years after his death and did so quite by accident. A few years back, a colleague who makes his living as a stand-up comedian and I were developing a corporate training series to teach first-time managers the basics of managing and motivating people. My friend Joey thought it might be a kick to base the series on the Three Stooges — sort of a spoof on the traditional leadership/management models.

It was during copious research on the subject that I stumbled upon the unexpected. The life of Moe Howard began to show classic signs of servant leadership. I was intrigued. I scoured the libraries and the Internet for information on Moe's life. I turned up a number of newspaper articles, a few scant biographical sketches, an autobiography, and a host of "stooge-ophile" Web sites containing various tidbits of information about Moe and his cohorts.

The deeper I dug into Moe Howard's life the more evidence of servant leadership I found. In researching Moe, I learned much about the practice of servant leadership and commitment to a vision and a cause. I learned a great deal about loyalty, too. I was truly moved. Also I discovered servant leaders can and do come from all walks of life, no matter how humble or bizarre their occupation or standing in life may be.

Servant leaders are not born leaders; they are just plain people, like you and like me — people who recognize what needs to be done, understand how to do it, and believe down to their very core that it will work, if they would only be given a chance to make it happen. What separates the servant leader from the masses however is the realization that chances are not things that are given, chances are things that we must take.

You already have what it takes to become a servant leader, to serve others by leading them toward their own independence, to use your unique talents and experience to identify the hidden needs of others and help them to meet those needs. If you dare to take a chance and step past the iron-clad beliefs that have been holding you back, you too may one day be counted among those who used their lives to make a positive difference in the world and who in return were rewarded with a life of wonder and joy, peace and prosperity, and the knowledge that your life mattered to someone other than yourself.

Everything you need is already within your reach; all you need do now is *take your chance.*

Part I

There's Gotta Be a Better Way!

CHAPTER 1

What Do You Want Out of Life?

If you are human and breathing, there is one dominating, universal fact that governs your life. You want something at this very moment. The truth is that we all want something nearly all of the time — more money, a newer car, a bigger or better place to live — and once we've filled our laundry list of material wants, we begin to long for less temporal things: security, peace of mind, better health, more free time, deeper meaning in our lives.

Ever since Mrs. Ug said to her husband, "Why don't we get out of this dump and look for a bigger cave," humans have been searching for a better way to get more of what they want out of life. For most of us, this search has centered itself smack in the middle of the way we've chosen to make a living.

As I observe those around me, though, a question comes to mind. If we've all been working and searching for such a long time, why is it so very few people ever seem to find what they are looking for? The answer is simple. They're looking in the wrong place or, more accurately, they've got the wrong focus.

When faced with the challenge of getting more out of life, most people go about their search in one of four ways. I break these ways down as:

- Wishing and hoping
- Winning at all costs
- Jack-of-all-trades syndrome
- The Big Lie

Wishing and Hoping: The most popular "method" people employ as a means of getting more of what they want out of life is to do little more than go to work, put in their time, then sit around wishing and hoping for good things to come their way. Wishin' and hopin' may make good song lyrics, but neither does a hoot to enhance the quality of our lives.

To achieve anything in life, we need to apply our resources (physical, mental, spiritual, and financial) to the very act of attaining it. Yet, this simple life truth seems to have gone unheeded by the majority. Over the years, I've read reports on studies that examine such things as the number of people who actually practice the age-old philosophy "You gotta give to get." These studies purport the average percentage of compliance to be as low as 10 percent. If you believe these studies, you'd have to believe most people go to work each day simply because that is what they did the day before. While at work, these same studies suggest, the majority of people have as their prime motivating focus finding ways to do less and less work, while getting paid more and more money. This extrapolates to an ultimate career goal of doing absolutely nothing, and collecting a big stack of money for doing so — politicians, incidentally, are the only animals who can apply this methodology and have it work.

I'm not sure of the actual numbers, but I do know that there is an army of people in our society who work only to retire, who feel that job satisfaction is a myth, who count the days till the weekend, and who have become convinced that the only way to wealth, happiness, and peace of mind is to win the lottery or become a game show contestant.

Winning at All Costs: On the flip side of wishing and hoping is the 110 percent effort method or more aptly named, the "winning at all costs syndrome." If you've ever watched a Saturday morning infomercial, I'm sure you're familiar with this one. Here the seeker of wisdom is told to focus on their goal and put 110 percent effort into attaining it. The most dangerous characteristic of this approach is that *it works.* I say dangerous, because practitioners of this method unwittingly find themselves sitting alone in the winners circle, with their life so distorted and out of balance they can hardly recognize it anymore. Most of these *winners* will find that they traded more of what *matters most* in life, for a few of the things that *matter least.*

The winning at all cost philosophy, although quite effective for short-term gain, is a very dangerous and counterproductive way of looking at life. There's no doubt in my mind that the blind acceptance of this myth of life, has led to the "epidemic" of panic attacks and anxiety disorders that seem to be plaguing our modern day society.

When we push ourselves to the breaking point, for too long a period of time, something has to give. This is common sense. Yet, this simple sense seems to elude so many would-be goal seekers.

The same people who push themselves to the breaking point in order to gather up more than the Joneses, or rise to the top of some social or corporate hierarchy, would never think of hopping into their luxury automobile and pushing the peddle to the floor never and letting up for anything or anyone until they reached their intended destination. They seem to easily understand this type of behavior will surely lead to the destruction of one of their most prized possessions, yet they have difficulty translating this same action into certain self-destruction.

Success, real success, cannot be determined by what you have, in comparison to what the other guy has, nor can it be expressed in any one value. We are not machines, designed to produce a single product. We are complex creatures, with physical, mental, spiritual, and financial needs. A life plan that neglects any or all of our human needs could never be good for us.

Jack of All Trades Syndrome: Next in the list of ineffective methodologies is what I like to call the Jack-of-all-trades Syndrome, which is nothing more than the 110 percent effort thing turned inside out. Here we hop from thing to thing, trying our hand at a little of this and a little of that.

The problem with this method is simple. Once a person begins a task, according to social scientists, his motivation for continuing will be determined by one of only two factors: to gain pleasure (he enjoys doing it) or to avoid pain (quitting will result in an unpleasant experience). In short, we commit to a thing only until it becomes difficult or unpleasant, at which point we abandon our efforts, in pursuit of an even shinier lure. As a result, we never spend the time necessary to become expert at a particular thing, which is a *sine qua non*, the essential ingredient in the attainment of success in any field. Like a fidgety novice investor, we end up pulling out, long before any significant return could be expected on our initial investment. The net result in transactions like these is at best a null one.

The Big Lie: The final method is a product of the "Me" generation. I call this method The Big Lie. It's nothing more than Joseph Campbell's "Follow your bliss!" with a twist. It's about picking what you like to do and doing it. This same myth has been popularized in a number of creative ways and on the pages of the hundreds of feel good, self-help books of our age.

Although there is some credence and measurable benefit to picking an occupation, vocation, or profession that yields you delight and ignites a fire inside your soul, the whole truth is, jumping into mud puddles all day long may make you happy, but it will yield little else including genuine reward and lasting rapture.

The fallout of the follow your bliss method lies all around us in the form of failed relationships and failed businesses. Doing what you enjoy without regard to the enjoyment or satisfaction of others, or without thought for whether what you are doing actually produces a product or service that is needed by anyone other than you, is only a recipe for disaster.

Like the novice prospector who falls prey to the alluring glitter of fool's gold, we too can be beguiled by the glimmer of what quenches our immediate desires and titillates our fantasies. But if we fall under its spell, and unwittingly settle for the consolation prize, we will surely miss the extraordinary opportunity that lies just beyond it.

The real riches of life, like nature's most abundant mineral reserves, lie below the surface and require some "educated digging" in order to uncover them. Simply chasing after *love or happiness, riches or joy, power or authority* and grabbing at it like it were the tail of a runaway dog never really works. In a private discussion regarding the reasons behind the unexpected success of his book *Man's Search for Meaning*, the late Dr. Viktor Frankl said, "Don't aim at success. The more you aim at it and make it a target the more you're going to miss it."[1]

Dr. Frankl never intended for his little book, which told of his plight as a prisoner in a Nazi death camp, to make such a huge shock wave around the world. In fact, he was apprehensive

[1] Frankl, Viktor E., Preface to *Man's Search for Meaning*. New York: Washington Square Press, 1985, pp. 16–17.

about even having his name appear on the title page. The author of some twenty more scholarly works, Frankl had little hope of success for this one. But this was the one that, ironically, achieved world fame for its author.

A great observer of life, Frankl learned a valuable lesson that helps us all. *What we pursue the most will surely become most elusive to us.* People who chase money will be poor all of their life. Those who grab at power and authority, like a spoiled child grabs for the last piece of candy, will rarely hold it for long. The moment the coveted prize is in their hands, greedy rivals begin their plot to take it from them. Money is a byproduct of valuable service and the only lasting forms of power and authority are those that are freely given to us by those whom we lead.

So then if hoping, focusing, sampling, or chasing won't get us what we are truly after, what then will?

There's Gotta Be a Better Way!

When I was nineteen years old, I supported a nasty and expensive habit I had acquired (the pursuit of a higher education) by driving a taxicab.

The dispatcher of the cab company was a surly character with the disposition of a junkyard dog and a set of personal hygiene habits to match. Each of my fellow cab drivers, as you might imagine, had his own little pet name for this colorful character. Her real name was Edna.

As far as I could tell, Edna had a passion for only two things in life . . . fresh jelly donuts and yelling obscenities at people. In truth, Edna's working vocabulary was limited to fifty words, forty-two of which couldn't be used in mixed company. But with the efficiency that usually accompanies economy, Edna made great use of the other eight. She arranged those other eight words in a number of very interesting and creative ways, but the one I believe she liked the best was this: "Yano kid...deres gotta be a betta way."

An old Hindu proverb reminds us that the greatest sources of wisdom often come packaged in homely wrappings. I'm not 100 percent sure, but I think those old Hindus had Edna in mind when they came up with that saying.

Putting Together the What, Why, and How

Have you ever wondered, in the quiet of your own thoughts, if there was some better way to get more of what you really want out of life? Well, a growing number of truly joyous and very successful people I know have proven that there is a better way, a much better way.

If you recall, I said earlier that the reason most people never seem to find what they are looking for is because they have the wrong focus. I realize one cannot make a statement like this without some sort of explanation, and the first part of that explanation must address the obvious subsequent questions: What is the *wrong focus*, and why is it so wrong?

To do a good job at answering these questions, I need to break the answer into three separate, yet inexorably linked parts. These three parts are the what, why, and how.

When we're finished, if you look back at our answers, you'll see a clear path between your present mindset and the one you'll need to develop in order to reach your personal and professional heights. From there, all you need do is follow the path, and like those who have gone before you, you'll be astonished and delighted at what you'll find.

Finding the Right Focus: What, Why, and How

Now let's get down to business. A good place to begin is with a thorough examination of the "what, why, and how" of finding the best strategy available to help us get more of what we want out of our business and our lives. The best place to begin is with the "what" of the equation. I think of the "what" as the thing or things we desire — the goal or prize.

Like we've already discovered, to be human is to want. Our unfulfilled wants create a longing emptiness — a void or vacuum within us, emanating from our very core. And, because nature abhors a vacuum, we are naturally driven to fill that void. Repeated, increasingly frantic, and ineffective attempts to fill our soul's void with material objects, loveless sex, mind numbing substances, or power and money only serve to drive us deeper and deeper into a darkened pit of despair.

Naturally, we begin to feel as if the failure we have experienced is our fault, that if we had only worked harder or longer, we might have gotten the fulfillment we seek, but that's not necessarily the case.

It really doesn't matter, how hard or furiously you work at a thing, or how good you become at performing a particular task, if the task you are performing or the work you're doing happens to be wrong. If you bake a lousy loaf of bread, what you might need is a new recipe. Baking more loaves, with the same bad recipe, will only yield more bad bread.

The philosophy that governs good bread baking also applies to business and to life itself. When things seem to be turning out badly, we might need to consider a new "recipe." One way to find that new recipe is to change the way we look at things.

Change Your Focus and Change Your Outcome

We have been taught to keep the object of our desire centered in the crosshairs as we pursue it. This teaching has become so much a part of our lives, we have developed a host of clever slogans like "Keep your eyes on the prize" to spur us along in our quest. Consequently, the picture we have firmly planted in our mind as we labor in our quest for fulfillment is the prize itself.

This may be a great technique for marksmen, but for most of life's goals it doesn't really work. The problem this creates is simple. We end up focusing so much of our attention on what it is we want that we have no room left in our thoughts for the things we need to do, be, and have in order to get what we want. Going back to our bread example for a moment, we all would like a steaming hot slice of delicious crusty bread, dripping with butter or glistening with sweet jam, but few want to take the time or perform the tasks involved in the mixing of the ingredients, the kneading and rising of the dough. We rarely invest the time necessary to bake our loaf to a golden brown in order that we might enjoy a taste of sweet success. And no matter how long we focus our attention on the photo of delicious bread, or conjure up memories of the aroma of baking bread, it won't materialize. The principles that govern the making of one kind of "dough" also seem to hold true for other kinds of dough.

For example, suppose I want to make more dough — more money for the work I do; I *want* a pay raise. Since people's salaries are typically based on what those paying them perceive their worth to be, if I have any hope of seeing a pay raise, I *need* to find ways of increasing my perceived worth to my employer. In short, I have to do more of the things that my employer perceives as being important to the growth and betterment of the organization and less of the things I think are important. Value is always a matter of perception.

For a few of you, the above morsel of truth may seem a bit "hard to swallow." However, I assure you that I make this statement based on many years of being on both sides of the employment equation, employer and employee. Truth be told, if your practice is to always ferret out the things that need to be done to make the organization you work for stronger and more profitable, you make yourself an indispensable part of that organization and thus increase your perceived value to the stewards of that organization. Do more of the things that matter most to the continued success of the organization, and do a lot more of them than you're paid to do, and you will eventually be paid a lot more for what you do if not by your present employer, then by someone a bit wiser.

For some reason, this simple truth evades most people seeking pay raises. They mistakenly feel that the road to higher earnings has something to do with drumming up the courage to march into the boss's office and demand more money..."or else!" In fact, this practice usually leads you down the highway to the unemployment line.

Focus on Needs Rather Than Wants

A better approach to higher wages might be to present your employer with a well thought out plan, one designed to substantially increase the organization's profits. It should be no mystery, although it usually is for some reason, the only way a company can pay out more money is to make more. Thus, if one is earnestly seeking a bigger share of the profit, one should find ways of enhancing and expanding it. But, in the main, most people get too caught up in what they want, to put any real thought into what they need to do so they may have what they want. We make a common, but natural, mistake when we focus on *wants* rather than *needs*.

All this is not to say that we don't keep our eyes on the prize. A prize, a goal, is imperative. Goals give us something to aim for; they establish reference points and destinations but goals alone are by no means a replacement for a good and dynamic plan that addresses what we must do in order to claim our prize, and the tenacious action we must take to fulfill that plan.

When a sales professional takes a revolving door approach to dealing with customers — *get 'em in, sell all you can, then get 'em out* — she unconsciously turns her *focus* away from what her real goal should be: identifying and meeting her customer's changing needs. By committing herself to serving the unique and developing needs of her clients, rather than treating customers like a never ending resource, the responsive salesperson insures the seeds of future business will germinate along with their long-term customer relationships. This, any seasoned businessperson will affirm, is an essential element in the building of wealth and the most profitable goal of any business relationship.

Long-term relationships can only be sired on a bed of trust, respect, and a mutual dedication to the benefits. These conditions are conceived the moment a committed businessperson puts aside her natural selfish need for instant gratification, the quick and easy sale, and works to uncover and meet the real needs of each of her customers, one at a time.

When you and I erroneously focus on how little we are appreciated or how underpaid we feel, more than on how we must improve our skills and perceived worth, we unconsciously undermine our desired goal by creating an environment counter to our goals. Self-pity causes us to do things like curse the ringing telephone that dares interrupt our lunch, or park in the spot closest to the door during inclement weather, leaving the customer out in the rain. When we opt for the quick sale over the chance to get to really learn about our customers' needs we end up focusing on *what we want* rather than *what we need to do to get what we want.*

13

It is important to establish a goal — a reference point, before we begin to take action, but it is equally important to focus on what we need to do, who we need to become, and what we need to have, in order for us to obtain that goal.

Take Action on Your Plans

Next, let's take a look at the "how" in the equation *the method* we choose to get what we desire. The word *method*, by definition, denotes action. Action is a good thing. Nothing happens without it.

No farmer in his right mind would expect to sit around waiting for corn seeds to drop from the sky like yesterday's rain, bury themselves in the soil, fight off insects and drought, and then, jump off the stalk and walk to market. Yet there are a host of otherwise rational and intelligent people who sit around dreaming up plans for a bigger and better money crop, only to never take action on those plans, and then they continue to wonder why nothing ever seems to improve in their life. The best plan of all is rendered impotent, unless and until someone takes action on it. Believe it or not, the first step toward maximizing our own returns is often to focus on giving rather than getting. Wait until you see the wild things that can happen when you begin to focus on giving instead of receiving.

CHAPTER 2

Survival of the Fittest? Maybe Not

When we take a closer look at the methods we usually employ to get more of what we want out of life, we can see a common thread running through all of them. That thread is selfishness. I used to think that selfishness (and its opposite, altruism) were purely human traits, until I was exposed to a different point of view — a gene's-eye view.

In his controversial book *The Selfish Gene* (Oxford University Press 1976), Dr. Richard Dawkins examines the biology of selfishness and altruism. Dr. Dawkins makes a great argument to support the biological predisposition of selfishness, right down to the genetic level. What this means is that we humans, along with all other living creatures on this planet, have in common a genetic coding that promotes the keeping of our own self-interest above that of anything else. We were born ruthlessly selfish, concludes Dr. Dawkins, and no matter how much we may deplore that fact, it does not stop it from being true.

Examining the relationship between the methods people employ to get what they want and their corresponding success rate from this new perspective proved enlightening. I realized that the majority of people who employ ruthless selfishness as their modus operandi never seem to catch and hold on to those things they have been chasing very long. They also end up living seemingly miserable existences, compared to those who adopt a more altruistic approach.

Looking at these two facts side by side, one might reasonably conclude there is an odd, apparently coincidental relationship between selfishness and a failure to attain our ultimate desires. I thought so too. That is, until I discovered, through even deeper digging into the research, there really is no coincidence. Dr. Dawkins, although it was not his original intent, actually proved the relationship between selfishness and misery and eventual extinction. Dr. Dawkins cites several behavioral studies designed to monitor the altruism and selfishness of birds, fish, and various other biological models.

These studies revealed an interesting chink in the accepted beliefs about self-preservation. The groups who acted in a selfish manner — meaning they tended to take what they wanted, when they wanted it, without any thought to giving anything back — although initially fairing better than the rest, actually ended up succumbing to disproportionate levels of disease and starvation and eventually died off much earlier. Those groups and species that exhibited the greatest levels of selfishness actually became extinct, and did so at an accelerated rate. In comparison, those groups that adopted altruistic behavior — the scientists termed this behavior "reciprocal" — tended, proportionately, to do far better in the long run compared to the mean. The scientists conducting these studies discovered that selfishness is not an insurance policy for survival, but rather a writ of execution (or more aptly, an act of suicide).

What I also found interesting in all of this was the illusion of prosperity cast in the short-term picture. In the short term, the selfish group faired much better than their altruistic counterparts — proving the accepted idea of survival of the fittest. No wonder so many of us fall into the trap of assuming the only way to get ahead is to beat others to the punch — to get our share first and damn the competition. We observe greed and selfishness working for others and adopt the same methods in our own lives. Eventually our eyes become fixed on the glitter of the here and now and blind to the long-term expense of our behavior. As we progress in our work together, however, I hope you will learn to question inherited core beliefs and by doing so discover the real truth behind the secret of long-term success, not to "survival" but to ultimate lasting success.

In order to really prosper — which for me means getting more than just one win, one time — we have to do more than just take from life; we have to give something back. For most people, the natural tendency to take and take, without giving anything back, is just too hard to resist.

A Legend about the Power of Giving

I recently heard a wonderful little fable from a leader of the Iroquois Confederacy that makes this point very well. Many years ago, the highlands were gripped by a terrible drought. The land was parched and cracked. The trees no longer bore fruit. Animals lay dead in the brown, sun-scorched fields. The streams dried up, taking with them the once abundant supply of fish. The people of the village were suffering as well. Most of the elders had perished from dehydration, and the children grew weaker with each passing sun. It was as if the gods were punishing the villagers for an evil that they had done.

Desperate, the shamans gathered on the highest hilltop, where they prayed to the gods for forgiveness and guidance.

After much praying, the gods answered: The people of the village had become too focused on worldly things. They took all that they could from the bountiful land until it could give no more. In all their taking they had not thought of giving something back to the land and to the gods who reigned over it. In response, the gods withheld the life-giving rain. The only hope for the village's survival was a sacrifice: the people of the village must make a burnt offering to the gods of their most prized possessions.

The shamans brought the news back to the villagers. The people were instructed to go to their homes and bring back their most-cherished possessions. The instructions were clear, but the souls of the people were not pure. How would the shamans know whether the offerings the villagers brought were indeed their most-prized possessions? Perhaps a substitute would do, something of value, but not their most-prized possession.

The next evening the villagers returned with their offerings, which the shamans took to the hilltop. The sacrificial fire burned throughout the night and bathed the village below with a red-yellow glow of hope.

The next morning, dark rain clouds appeared over the hilltop where the sacrificial fires had burned. The clouds began moving over the village. Distant sounds of thunder called the people from their shelter. All looked to the sky in anticipation of the renewal of life.

The villagers watched in disbelief as a single raindrop fell and disappeared instantly as it touched the parched earth. The clouds then gave way to the bright summer sun, whose rays were stronger and hotter then ever before. A cry resounded from the village. How could the gods forsake them like this! What would become of them and their children?

A young girl no older than five witnessed this scene. Her youthful heart was pure. She had heard the shamans speak of sacrifice to the elders. She had witnessed the pain and suffering of the other children. The little girl thought for a moment: What might she offer to the gods? As she pondered the question, a vision appeared before her, and at once she knew what she must do.

That evening, the little girl went to the hilltop, where the embers of the sacrificial fires still smoldered. She took with her a small sack made of hide, the top of which was gathered and held tightly by a string of hemp.

When she arrived at the hilltop, she knelt before the embers and opened her package. From the sack she pulled a small doll, a warrior dressed in blue deerskin with a beautiful headdress made of blue robin's feathers. It was her doll, her only possession, and she loved it with all her heart and soul.

She kissed the doll one last time then laid it on the pile of golden embers. Tears ran down her face as she looked to the heavens, asking the gods to accept her offering and bring life once again to her people. Tired from her long journey, she laid her head down on the cold earth and slept.

The warmth of the morning sunshine woke the little girl. She wiped the sleep from her eyes, and as her vision cleared she was treated to the most magnificent sight she had ever witnessed. Little blue flowers . . . as far as the eye could see. They covered the hilltop and flowed into the valley. The little blue flowers caressed her skin as she reached out to touch them in disbelief and tickled her feet as she ran back to her village, laughing all the way.

The villagers listened to her story with guilt. The purity of her selfless act exposed the dark shadows of their own self-centeredness. One by one, the elders of the village went to their homes and emerged with their arms full of the things that they once had coveted. Together with the shamans, they went to the hilltop and returned some of their gifts to the gods so that they might make room for more. As the fires returned the treasures to the earth, the rains came once again.

To put this legend into more familiar terms, I'd like to turn to a fellow by the name of Eugene. Although he would have described himself as a simple man, Eugene had a powerful philosophy when it came to maximizing his bounty in life. He put it this way: "You can't receive anything with a closed hand. You must first let go of what you have clutched in your hand, you must give before you can ever receive a thing."

There's nothing really evil about selfishness, or "self-centeredness," as I prefer to call it. It's simply nature's way of ensuring the survival of the species. But, that's about all it will insure, basic survival — nothing more, nothing less.

If we concentrate all of our efforts on getting our basic needs met, we will surely succeed. However, if we concern ourselves only with meeting our instinctual needs, we can expect a lifetime of basic, minimal returns — which is nothing more than basic survival. If we want more, we have to work against nature and broaden our focus to include serving the needs of others, and allowing them the opportunity to serve ours.

We must give in order to receive, and we must serve others' needs in addition to our own. Not exactly earth shattering, is it? It's not a new lesson, and many of us learn it on our own. In fact, this message of service to others is the cornerstone of virtually every major religion; prophets and philosophers have touted it throughout history. Even present-day philosophers like Zig Ziglar, one of the finest sales trainers of our century, refers to it when he says, "You can have everything in life you want if you will just help enough other people get what they want."

You gotta give to get: A principle easy to express but far more difficult to act on, especially when things are going wrong, when we feel underpaid or underappreciated, when life deals us a bad hand. At such times, we tend to become less concerned with meeting the needs of others and more concerned with our own, selfish needs. If I'm starving to death, I don't care that your steak dinner was served cold.

We can't change our genetic predisposition, but we can, through repeated, concentrated effort, upset our genetic design. Once we become successful in our efforts, we'll be at a place where we are able to *help others as a means of helping ourselves*, a sort of a genetic compromise.

Do Unto Others — Not!

The truth is, getting to the point where we are willing to serve the needs of others is only half of the challenge. The other half of the challenge comes in *knowing exactly what it is that we are supposed to give* so that we may have our own needs met. Coincidentally, this is the exact spot where most people make the same catastrophic mistake.

Because we look at life through genetically selfish eyes, we end up mistaking *our needs for the needs of others*. No surprise really. After all, we're only following instructions. You know the instructions I'm talking about, they're in a thing called the Golden Rule, "Do unto others...yada, yada, yada." Okay, maybe that's not exactly how it goes, but you get my drift. The problem is, if we follow the above advice verbatim, we're sure to screw up!

The traditional interpretation of the Golden Rule makes one wrong assumption: that we are all alike. In fact, quite the opposite is true: We are as different as we are alike. Sure, as a species, we have a lot of the same needs, like the need to be loved and to belong, the need for food and shelter, the need for safety and security. We even behave in the same predictable ways and have many of the same likes and dislikes. Yet we are all different from one another, in that each of us has different dreams, wants, and desires. We each have a unique set of inherited talents, skills, and cultural experiences. Although we are all moving through life together, each of us is traveling his or her own separate path and at different rates of speed, with dynamic needs unlike those of any other. Assuming that I can meet your needs with the same solutions that I use to meet my own is a little like the guy who gave his wife a *Sports Illustrated* swimsuit calendar for her birthday. It gets an effect, but not necessarily the one he was hoping for.

The only sure way of getting what we want lies in our ability to serve others, by identifying and meeting their legitimate needs, and doing so in a way that is best for them. But if we confuse what they need with what we want, the only thing we'll end up with is failure.

When you really think about it, maybe all that's needed is a new Golden Rule. Hey, I've got it! Try this one on for size: *Never offer your comb to a bald man!*

When we offer our comb to a bald man, nobody wins. We lose, because no matter how much time and energy we have spent in the process of "trying to help," the needs of the other person remain unmet. As if that's not bad enough, our failed actions have caused irreparable harm to our relationship with another human being. Like pouring salt into an open wound, our good intentions serve at best only to diminish the other person's hope of ever finding an answer to the problem, and at worst cause further harm. We both leave the encounter a bit weaker. Not a pretty picture, but it happens all the time.

When we act on our natural instinct and take a self-centered approach to serving others' needs, the best outcome we can expect is a null one. The shopkeeper who only stocks "regular sizes" loses out on all those big and tall, petite and small customers. The man who confuses his want of a bigger home and newer car with his family's need to have him by their side as they mature and develop, risks losing a boat-full of wonderfully fulfilling relationships and memories, the likes of which can't be bought at any price. The parents who determine their child's vocation based on "what's best for her" rob the world of a talented new star. The lawyer who pushes to win her case at all costs puts her own needs ahead of her client's, and as a result serves neither. The doctor whose ego will not let him admit that he lacks the proper experience to best treat his patient ends up doing more harm than any disease ever could.

Move from a Self-Centered Focus
to a Visionary Focus

We call the person who sees beyond the obvious a "visionary." All it takes for us to become a visionary is to expand our focus from the needs we see in our own reflection to the needs emerging in others. When we look at a common situation through a visionary's eyes quite the opposite of the effects described above holds true. Take for instance a recent experience that happened at a uniform and gift specialty chain, appropriately named Just for Nurses. After the managers and employees of the business were exposed to this new way of thinking, strange things began to happen: Sales went through the roof!

The idea behind the burgeoning retail chain was a good one: to serve a small segment of the general population with anything and everything that they needed or desired. Things were going well, better than expected really. Nurses from ninety miles away made special trips to visit the little boutique, located in an out of the way area. The managers of the store selected only the newest and hottest fashions in uniforms. They kept a more than adequate supply of merchandise in sizes ranging from extra small to tall and very large.

In addition to the usual paraphernalia associated with the practice of nursing — reference books, stethoscopes, blood pressure apparatuses, and other medical thingamabobs — they boasted one of the largest selections of gifts and collectibles in the industry. They had thought of everything, or so they believed.

Indeed, the managers of this fine establishment were delivering superior customer service, and they were addressing a lot of the "wants" their customers expressed, such as trendy uniforms, convenient shopping hours, unique and hard to find gift items. As the managers soon found out, however, not all of a person's real needs are that obvious. Not until they began to view their customers' needs through a visionary's eye were they able to see that something was missing. Shortly after everyone in the company was introduced to the principles outlined in this book, I was standing in their store when the following scene unfolded.

A woman entered the store with her three-year-old son in tow. She was greeted in the usual fashion, the highlights of the store were pointed out, and she was given a quick tour of the latest fashions. She was then set free to explore to her heart's content, and she immediately began her hunt for buried treasure on the sales racks.

Quickly bored from a lack of his mother's attention, the little tyke began to amuse himself by swinging from clothes racks like they were a jungle gym. Tiring of that, he headed straight for a display of delicate figurines.

Mom caught sight of the impending disaster. She dropped an armful of expensive designer uniforms, crossed the entire length of the store in only three strides, and snatched the little darling by the elbow, none too soon I might add.

As her face turned toward me, I could see a familiar look of embarrassment, tinted with shades of anger and frustration. Mortified, she looked around for the door. As she did, the sales clerk cut off her path and asked her son a magic question: "Do you like puzzles?"

That got the attention of both mother and son. "Yes," he chimed back. Looks of excitement, make that "relief," suddenly filled the faces of everyone in the store, including me.

The sales clerk pulled a brand-new jigsaw puzzle out from somewhere behind the counter. She removed the cellophane from the box, sat on the floor with the little guy, and began to put the puzzle together. I turned to see the mother's reaction but only caught a glimpse of the back of her head as she disappeared into the dressing room, both arms filled with clothes.

The end result was a purchase of more than $400 by a woman who had one foot out the door. And the little terror...ugh, I meant to say *the little darling*...got a free puzzle out of the deal.

I asked the salesperson what made her do what she had done. She said, "I could see that poor woman clearly wanted and needed to get new uniforms for herself. The uniform she had on was certainly well worn. But I could also see another, even greater need. She needed someone to occupy her child while she tended to her own needs. I just did what I thought I should do," she said. "Come to think about it," she added, "I really didn't think about it; I just responded, I guess."

When I asked her if she had purchased the puzzle with that use in mind, she just chuckled and shook her head. "I picked that puzzle up for my niece on my way to work this morning. The thing only cost me five bucks, but it just earned me forty-five in commission," she said with a smile and a wink.

I wonder how many uniform shops that woman walked out of before she visited one staffed by a servant-centered salesperson and got what she was really looking for?

I guess you could say both customer and salesperson made out well in the encounter, not to mention the managers, stockholders, and other employees of the establishment, who will no doubt benefit from the "found money." When a person begins serving the needs of the world in ways that, up until that moment, have gone unfilled, magic happens!

Developing the Proper Mind-set

We've just touched on the need to transform our mode of viewing life's events from self-centered eyes to what I referred to as a visionary's eyes. This transformation aids us in discerning the difference between our own legitimate needs and those of another. This new focus also prepares us to adopt a new perspective with which to effectively interpret age-old life situations. Armed with this new understanding, we are better able to extrapolate the legitimate needs of others from the data we collect, through general observations and specific inquiries. All of this helps to insure we will never again offer our comb to a bald man. To put it a bit more succinctly: with the proper mind-set, we can uncover the unmet needs of others simply by watching what they do, asking questions, and listening to answers.

More times than not, the adoption of a visionary's mind-set requires us to take a proactive leadership role in identifying and meeting the legitimate needs of another person; not only are we required to uncover the need, but we must also lead the person into adopting the solution. For instance, we all have one of those friends who is forever seeking advice to resolve one life dilemma or another but never applies the advice we, or for that matter anyone else, offer them. After a while, our self-centered outlook prompts us to *stop wasting our valuable time,* so we simply respond by never again offering this person another bit of advice. When we look at the same situation through a visonary's eyes, we might discover that the reason our friend fails to act on our "valuable" advice is because all along we have been telling him what *we* would do if *we* were in his situation. Our self-centered focus has caused us, once again, to offer our comb to a bald man without ever giving thought to how our friend should best solve his problem given his unique and specific set of needs.

Our friend does not need our rendition of what we would do if we were in his shoes; he needs us to lead him through the steps of solving his own dilemma, taking into account his preferred outcome, not the outcome we would hope for if we were in his situation. This type of behavior takes far more commitment to our friendship than our usual pontificating does, but the outcome both we and our friend can expect as a result will be far more beneficial than if we had not made the commitment: our friend not only gets his problem solved and grows as a person in the process; we gain the satisfaction of knowing we have helped another person deal effectively with his problems, plus a bucketful of free time formerly eaten up listening to him gripe and complain. In this example, as in many other cases, we find ourselves *serving* another by *seeing* an underlying need of theirs, and *leading* them to help themselves.

Robert K. Greenleaf was perhaps the first to popularize the term "servant leadership" in his 1977 book of the same name, and various contemporary business models recommend "visionary leadership." However, the concepts are far from new. Moses served those he led by leading them on a forty-year hike

through the desert, making each of them stronger, more independent, and better able to serve others through their experience. And, although the various definitions of "visionary" or
"servant" leadership may differ in many respects from mine, I
find these terms to be complementary and useful in describing
the type of person who serves the needs of others as a means of
personal fulfillment. Therefore, for purposes of brevity and
clarity, I will use the term *servant leader* when referring to a person who has adopted a servant-centered mind-set and a visionary approach to identifying and meeting the legitimate needs of
others as a method of getting more of what he or she wants out
of life.

In the following chapter, we will begin to define and examine the characteristics of a servant leader in order to establish a
benchmark for the development of our own thinking and
behavior.

CHAPTER 3

Portrait of a Servant Leader

The role of a servant leader requires a unity of mind, body, and spirit, a rounded life full of diverse experience and understanding, a life of universal utility. This type of life can't be obtained by focusing all of our efforts, talents, and resources on the attainment of any monolithic goal. There are four basic dimensions to the life of every servant leader: physical, mental, financial, and spiritual. Each dimension plays an important part in the servant leader's ability to identify and meet the needs of others. Without abundance in each of these areas, the servant leader will not be able to carry out his or her role effectively.

In studying the lives and actions of servant leaders and in the examination of my own successes and failures at living a servant-centered life, I have observed that no other critical measure is more important in determining the character of a servant leader than balance. Maintaining balance between the physical, financial, mental, and spiritual dimensions of life is essential as we approach building abundance. Focusing too much attention on the development of a single element of a servant leader's character will only serve to diminish the remaining three.

The single-minded actions we have used in the past for the purposes of short-term gain will get us nowhere toward developing the character and mind-set of a servant leader. We could spend the rest of our lives in pursuit of a particular summit, and even if we attain it, we might end up serving society only as peculiar curiosities. I was reminded of this fact recently as a close friend shared an experience he and his two young sons had just had.

As soon as they were old enough to appreciate the experience, my friend Kevin returned to mainland China to introduce his two sons to their heritage. Part of that trip involved a day-long trek up a mountain to visit a Buddhist temple and the monks that inhabited it. As they viewed the monks in a state of meditation, Kevin proudly shared the fact that a monk could, by spending the majority of his waking day in meditation over many years, attain such a high degree of control over his body that he could slow his respirations and heart rate to a point of near death and maintain this state for hours on end. "Gee dad, if you spent your whole life meditating, wouldn't you miss out on a lot?"

Out of the mouths of babes. . . . Through his young son's innocent observations, Kevin was able to see a truth that often eludes conscious thought: We tend to desire only those things that we ourselves lack. And, in this unspoken truth, Kevin was able to find an answer to a problem he wasn't even aware he had developed.

For over a decade and a half, Kevin had been living, in his own words, "free from the crushing hold of Communism." He worked long hours and saved virtually every penny he made to amass what, as a young child living in China, he would have considered to be an unattainable fortune, even though by American standards he was earning only a modest income. Even though Kevin and his family were enjoying a comfortable lifestyle, Kevin always wanted more. Sadly, he had fallen into the same trap many do, mistakenly comparing his own rightful success with that of the elite whose stories grace the pages of the business and tabloid magazines. Kevin soon developed an obsession with financial success. He began to work longer and harder than ever before, and did so at the expense of his relationships with his family and friends, his health, and his spiritual peace of mind.

Standing there in front of the monks that he so admired for their heightened sense of spirituality, and forced to respond to his son's innocent question, Kevin strained to make sense of his own life's quest. "Fifteen years ago I lacked money, so I made the accumulation of riches my life's mission. Today I have money and I yearn for the spirituality I lost along the way to financial gain. I now know what I really needed in my life was neither riches nor spirituality, but a balance of all things."

We need to keep in the forefront of our mind the concept of balance in all things that we do. That said, let's take a closer look at one servant leader's life.

Moses, Portrait of a Servant Leader

To bring the traits and qualities of a servant leader to life, I offer as an example the story of Moses. Nope, not that Moses: the Moses I'm referring to is Moses Horwitz, born Moses Harry Horwitz in Brooklyn, New York, fourth in a row of male siblings: Irving, Jack, Sam, and Moses. You'll no doubt remember him better as Moe Howard, leader of the wildest comedic trio in American entertainment history, the Three Stooges.

One hallmark of the servant leader is a proclivity to focus

attention on others. This particular quality surfaced at a young age in Moe. Preceded by three brothers, Moe was supposed to have been a girl, or so Jessup the butcher prophesied. In fact, as a young boy, Moe was often mistaken for a girl. By age four, his hair had grown into a mass of long beautiful curls, the source of much teasing from all.

In September of 1903, at the age of six, Moe started school. Each school day began with his mother waking him half an hour before everyone else so she could wind his hair into long, shoulder-length finger curls. This daily ritual gave his mother a great deal of pleasure, but you can imagine the effect Moe's long curly locks had on his classmates.

From the very first day, Moe fought his way to and from P. S. 101 in the Bath Beach section of Bensonhurst, New York. He fought battle after battle because of his curls, yet he always seemed to resist cutting off the locks that brought so much delight to his mother. Resist he did, until one sunny spring afternoon when he stood, scissors in hand, hacking away at the source of his frustration. Once the passion of the moment had receded, Moe's thoughts turned to his mother. What had he just done? He had ruined one of his poor mother's simple pleasures.

Devastated by his realization, Moe hid under the porch of his Brooklyn home in an attempt to forestall the inevitable. Finally discovered by his frantic father, he emerged from under the porch and caught sight of his mother. Their eyes locked, his mother's gaze drifted to the top of Moe's head. She was the first to break the silence: "Thank God you did it," she said softly in her guttural European accent, "I didn't have the courage."

All along, Moe's mother knew that the curls were the source of her son's troubles, but ironically, she thought he liked them and didn't want to hurt him by cutting them off. By assuming that we know what the needs of another are, we often get ourselves into trouble and make the matter worse. But, as is often the case with the servant leader, the pain Moe suffered as a result of his good intentions did not go unrewarded. Both Moe's trademark haircut and legendary wise-guy persona can easily be traced to his tumultuous boyhood. *Many times, our greatest rewards are simply the positive offspring of a painful experience.*

The Birth of a Servant Vision

Times were rough for Moe and his family, as they were for many immigrant families of their time. Young Moe witnessed firsthand the struggle to survive. Yet even as a young boy, Moe's insight seemed to allow him to see something more — a powerful phenomenon inherent in the immeasurable power of laughter as a poultice for life's greatest setbacks and tragedies.

From an early age, Moe hoped to become a messenger of joy. According to his memoirs, Moe felt that making people laugh was his gift to others. In late May of 1914, Moe picked up a copy of *Billboard* magazine and read an ad that would bring him closer to fulfilling his mission. The ad read: "Wanted! Young man, average height, to play juvenile parts and do general business. Must have own wardrobe. Send photo. If necessary, can send fare. Capt. Billy Bryant, the showboat *Sunflower*, Dockside 8, Jackson, Mississippi."

No doubt, in Moe's mind this ad was written just for him, but in reality Moe had a few problems. At the time, he wasn't quite eighteen, he stood only five feet, four inches, and the closest thing he had to a "wardrobe" was an old, tattered suit that belonged to his older brother Jack. With the prodigious confidence often exhibited by a servant leader in pursuit of a vision, Moe figured that if he only could meet Capt. Billy Bryant face to face, he could convince the captain to hire him.

This blind leap of faith, against logic and the advice of

friends, epitomizes the extraordinary trust exhibited by servant leaders in fulfillment of their mission. They truly believe that things will work themselves out, even if the situation seems hopeless right from the start. It is this trust and faith, I believe, that makes them immune to the obstacles that lie in the path of any worthwhile goal. This same faith seems to allow the servant leader to arrive at creative solutions to problems that inevitably crop up along the way. As a rule, their creativity borders on the wacky — making no sense to anyone but themselves. Moe Howard was no exception.

The story has it that as Moe paced the room pondering a way to overcome his shortcomings, a photograph hanging on the wall caught his eye. The photo was of a neighbor, Arthur Brandon. Brandon fit the description in the ad quite well. He was a handsome young man of medium build with a good physique and a full head of dark wavy hair. Moe got an idea — which for a servant leader on a mission can be dangerous. He sent the photo of his neighbor to Captain Billy, pretending he was the fellow in the picture. Moe figured that the good captain would be impressed enough by the combination of Brandon's looks and Moe's résumé to give him the job.

When Moe confided his off-the-wall plan for entering show business to his brother Sam (more commonly known as Shemp), Shemp thought Moe had taken leave of his senses. In expected fashion, Shemp reeled off a litany of logical reasons why Moe should scrap the whole idea — and Moe listened but paid no attention. Servant leaders seem to know exactly what they must do, and once their mind is made up, there seems to be no stopping them.

Like any leader with a vision, Moe's actions appeared to be quite *illogical*, even perhaps irrational to those closest to him. The closest and most-trusted allies of the servant leader often express the most vehement opposition. They do so, I believe, out of concern for the welfare of the servant leader. This lack of support by others is rarely, if ever, enough to dissuade servant leaders from carrying out their original plan.

The odd part of this whole process is that it always seems to work out: the particulars of the original scheme may not always remain intact, but the outcome tends to meet or exceed the expectations of the leader's original vision, as it would in Moe's fledgling career as an actor.

Following what must have been a really awkward introduction to his new boss — and I'm sure I am understating the emotional magnitude of the encounter — Moe auditioned for, got, and subsequently played the part magnificently.

There is a driving force behind a servant leader's pursuit of a vision. Most speak of this invisible force as if it were a double-edged sword, with a carrot dangling on one side and a sleep-interrupting, nagging admonition on the other — both combining to hasten the servant leader toward the fruition of her vision and keep her from giving up.

This force of faith arms the servant leader with a sense of purpose that is so intense she becomes invulnerable to the army of naysayers, critics, and antagonists who forever dwell in the way of new ideas.

As servant leaders make headway, their efforts are rewarded by a powerful sense of purpose. This sense of purpose results in what a casual onlooker might call bullheaded determinism. This unwavering tenacity is the engine that drives servant leaders on when all logic tells them to give up. Tenacity and an unshakable faith are perhaps the only things that keep servant leaders going during times of great personal sacrifice and through the long periods of loneliness many servant leaders experience in their quest.

Things Are Sometimes Just As Bad As They Seem

Moe Howard exhibited that sense of purpose in the relentless pursuit of his first acting job. But as strong as his purpose was then, it paled in comparison to what it would become in the years that followed. Early in their comedy career, Moe and his brother Shemp began an act on the vaudeville circuit, billing themselves as Howard and Howard. Their first gig was a three-day stint at the Majestic Theater in Manhattan during which they were hired to perform comedy relief.

The stage manager signaled their first performance by yelling down to their rat-infested dressing room, "Howard and Howard — up and at 'em!" The curtain opened and the brothers walked on stage, where they were met by the sound of a single person applauding. The show went downhill from there.

Less than two minutes into their act people began walking out. This continued until all three hundred seats were vacant and Moe and Shemp, with five minutes still left in their routine, continued to play, to an empty theater. When they finished, they each took a bow and left the stage.

Moe and Shemp subsequently learned that they had been hired as "a clean-up act." At the time, people often sought shelter from the bitter cold by going to the theater. You could plunk down your nickel, the price of a ticket, and keep warm and entertained all day long. Since a theater's profits were based on the turnover of seats, when the theater manager at the Majestic saw that the theater was packed, he would open the basement door and yell "Howard and Howard — up and at 'em." The brothers would do their act, the audience would walk out, and so it went: for six more shows that day, nine on Saturday, and eight on Sunday. It's not hard to imagine how painful and humiliating the experience must have been, but with a vision firmly planted in their minds, they never gave up.

Stick to the Vision and Things Begin to Happen

Once a servant leader proves unwavering commitment to his vision, he begins to attract to his cause other servant leaders, who are themselves often on a mission. Often these servant leaders appear from out of the blue, as if they were somehow being directed by an overseeing force. Many appear in unlikely forms: a child, a stranger, a former foe turned friend. Help and emotional support may also show up in something as simple as the lyrics to a song.

Moe's mission to heal the world with laughter was nurtured by visits and acts of support of many other servant leaders, who often arrived on the scene with an uncanny sense of timing.

Was That a Paradigm I Just Heard Shifting?

Sometimes all we need to knock us off the horse of routine thinking is a little nudge. My hope is that I've been successful in my attempt to nudge you a bit, enough in fact to cause you to challenge your old beliefs about the best ways to achieve success in life and in business.

My guess is, that at this point, you're probably thinking that there might be something to this servant leader mumbo jumbo. Well, if I did my job right, you should be challenging, at least just a bit, your well established "success" practices. It may be becoming clear to you that the old accepted definitions of "success" are not as shiny and bright in the light of wisdom cast by this new age as they were once touted to be. You may even be beginning to see that in order to attain what you personally would define as success — something much more substantive than the monolithic ideals of the past — you need to abandon outdated, ineffective methods and replace them with ones that can actually help you attain your vision for the future. If you want to get the most you can out of your life, and do it in a way that will satisfy your body, enrich your mind, and comfort your soul, you must learn to use your talents, your unique experiences, and finely tuned skills to identify and meet the needs of as many people as you can. It's as simple as that. The more needs you can identify and meet, the bigger and more fulfilling your own reward will be. What also might be becoming evident is how unexpectedly complex this business of *identifying and serving the needs of others* really can be. As simple as it all appears on the outside, it can be a formidable bear to wrestle with. Fear not! I'm here to help, and I've got a plan.

CHAPTER 4

Learning What It Takes to Serve

A re you ready to tackle the next phase of living as a servant leader? Well, I've got some good news and some bad news. The good news is you are already light-years ahead of the crowd. The moment you snatched this book from the shelf you took action on improving your life, and in doing so you separated yourself from the hordes of people who will continue to do nothing more than wish and hope for their lives to change.

Now for the bad news for those of you who resist change like it was an express bus to hell: There are a number of changes you need to make in order to prepare yourself to identify and serve the needs of others. You are going to be asked to change how you approach your work, your relationships with others; you'll be asked to change the way you view your past and the events that have worked to shape your life. You may even have to alter your plans for the future. In addition, the work you are going to be called to do may be difficult and often frustrating. You may come to find, as others have who have taken this road before you, that many of the views you have held, actions you have taken, thoughts you have had, and beliefs you have harbored are not as appropriate as you once thought. Although it might not be apparent, when it comes to matters of self-improvement, most people never make it past the stage you are in now: They habitually cling to the familiar yet destructive behavior that has caused them so much anguish in the past. Like the alcoholic who reaches for her next drink despite the fact that she is consciously destroying her life, people cling to the familiar as if it were a life raft. I call this behavior futile acceptance: *this is the way my life has always been and this is the way it will always be.* But it doesn't have to be. All you need to change your life is the willingness to do so, a plan, and the faithful tenacity to see that plan through.

Of course, the way may not always be smooth. It's perfectly normal to feel frustration and heightened emotions when we are learning something new. When we take the path of serving the needs of others as a means of serving our own needs, we are breaking away from nature, and because we are, everything we do is going to seem, well, "unnatural." Developing a mind-set that allows you to identify and serve the needs of others is initially going to feel unnatural. But the feelings you will face are no different from those you have experienced when you learned to ride a bike, attempted to speak a new language, or tried to write with your nondominant hand. When we do these things, we are breaking from our natural behavior, and the act produces a strong negative response in us — like we are somehow doing something wrong.

So remember, avoid giving in to the negatives. Just as when you learned to ride a bike, stick with it, fix your attention on the exhilaration and joy of doing something new and exciting, and remember, I'll be right behind you — cheering you on. Let's take a moment now to talk about what's ahead.

Like those first attempts to master riding a bicycle, during the journey we are about to begin you're going to become frustrated and frightened at times. You may even suffer a few bumps and bruises along the way. I'm also pretty certain that, out of your frustration, you, like many people I've worked with, will be prompted to call me dirty names — go right ahead, I'm used to it by now. When things get really rough, you may also feel like chucking the towel into the ring and calling it quits: you're not alone in this either.

Bumps and bruises are inevitable byproducts of learning and strangely enough, those of us with the will to go on naturally accept them as such. What throws us off the track more than anything else however, is the feeling that we are not making headway, and so here are some guidelines to help you see that you are progressing.

The Four Stages of Learning Any New Skill

Serving the needs of other people involves, for most of us, the mastery of a whole new set of skills. Educators say that as we learn to master a new skill, we make our way through a series of four stages that begin with incompetence and end with mastery. The four stages are:

1. unconscious incompetence,
2. conscious incompetence,
3. conscious competence, and
4. unconscious competence.

In the first stage we simply don't know what it is we don't know. An example of this stage can be found in a newborn baby. There are so many tasks a baby needs to master in order to live safely and happily, yet babies have no idea that they even need to know these things.

In the second stage of learning, *conscious incompetence*, we discover that there is something we don't know how to do. For example, as babies we had no concept of bicycles — and the joy of riding them. As we grew, we learned about bicycles and the pleasure they seemed to bring to the kids who knew how to ride them. As a result, our interest in learning to ride a bike was piqued.

Do you remember your first attempt to ride a two-wheeled bicycle? Does the phrase "No! Get away from me with that stuff — it stings!" jog your memory? At that point, you discovered there was something you wanted to do, but didn't know how to do it. This is the point where you are now.

You have perhaps known that what you've been doing to build a life and make a living has not worked out the way you originally intended. You may also have been harboring a suspicion that some better way might exist to enable you to live a decidedly better life. But up until the moment you reached for this book on the shelf, you had no idea what that way was, let alone what magic it would hold for you once you learned to master it. It was at this point that you became consciously aware of your own incompetence.

Before we can even think about learning a new set of life skills that will enable us to identify and meet the needs of others, there are a few critical steps we must take to prepare ourselves to meet the inevitable challenges.

The first step in the self-development process involves identifying the personal traits and behaviors that are common to the people who have mastered the art and science of serving others as a means to improving the quality of their lives.

Next in the process is spending time and energy to build a solid personal foundation from which you will eventually be called to serve. This is where the process begins of developing your strengths in the four specific life areas mentioned in the previous chapter — physical, mental, spiritual, and financial. These four areas hold the resources you will need when you begin supporting others in their own quest to meet their needs.

Since you can't give what you yourself lack, you will have to construct a foundation capable of supporting not only your needs, but also the demanding and constantly changing needs of others. The greater and more solid your foundation, the more people you will eventually be able to help. The more people you help, the greater you own reward will be.

There is, however, one caveat. There will come a point in the future when you can use the new skills and habits you have acquired with growing efficiency. It is at this critical juncture when you will pass into stage three of the learning process: *conscious competence*. Here, we have achieved a certain level of competency, we can do something new, but we must make a conscious effort to do it. This is similar to the point where you found yourself riding your bike, straight, erect, and on your own steam; but you had to concentrate with every ounce of your being.

A word or two of caution is in order for what potentially might derail you as you reach this juncture on your new learning track. As you progress in the learning process, and your ability to actually get through some of the new tasks without stumbling and falling grows, you're going to be tempted to jump ahead and rush to apply your newfound knowledge in real-life situations before you're ready. Don't. I stress this because I have found, even in myself, a propensity to want to jump ahead to the "fun stuff" and leave behind the boring and often arduous task of preparation. If you jump ahead without taking the time to develop an adequate surplus of physical, mental, spiritual, and financial energy, you are going to fail. It's that simple.

Applying the principles you are about to learn before you are adequately prepared will cause you to inadvertently slip back into the 110 percent mind-set: concentrating entirely on building one element of your life — financial, for instance — at the expense of the other three. When this happens, we find our lives critically out of balance; perhaps we become ill, bankrupt, mentally and spiritually drained, or depressed. Other times, we simply overstress ourselves by trying to give others what we lack ourselves. The result is we quickly find ourselves actually resenting the very people we started out to help: *All I do is sacrifice myself for the sake of others. I'm getting tired of giving and giving, without ever getting anything in return.* Either way, you are going to find yourself in a weakened position, at which point it makes perfect sense to quit. This is the point of failure.

You can avoid this kind of failure by taking the time to build a strong, solid foundation, paying equal attention to each of the four elements (physical, mental, spiritual, and financial) and making sure no one element takes precedent over any other — and by resisting the tendency to rush ahead of your forever-growing ability to serve. A building erected on a lopsided foundation, or one without sufficient strength, will eventually weaken and fall. The same result can be expected if you try to build your servant leader life on a weak foundation.

The fourth and final stage of learning seems to arrive without fanfare. This stage, *unconscious competence*, finds us riding our new bike, full tilt: ringing the bell, waving at neighbors, and whistling a happy tune. We are in total control of our bicycle and expertly piloting it through the neighborhood without giving the matter a second thought. At some point in the future, you will realize that you are going about the business of identifying and serving the needs of others as if it were second nature. At that time it will be — a second nature, that is.

So, let's continue with our discussion of learning and examine what we need to do in order to start enjoying the benefits found in identifying and serving the needs of others.

Part II

Preparing Yourself to Serve

CHAPTER 5

You Can't Sell from an Empty Cart

B efore we can begin thinking about serving the needs of others, it is important to take a tip from nature — that's right, the same nature that ensures our basic survival by making us self-centered — and make certain that you are strong enough to do so. A common mistake I've seen along the way is for people to jump ahead and try to serve others before they're ready. You simply can't do it — and expect a good outcome, that is.

I was reminded of the part this essential principle plays in our success this very morning as I sat on a plane bound for New York, listening to the flight attendant give her standard pre-flight briefing. You know the briefing I'm talking about; it's the one nobody listens to — about how to put on your seat belt, where the airplane exits are, and so forth. The part of her speech that is the most applicable to our discussion is the part about what to do in the "unlikely event that the plane loses cabin pressure."

At the beginning of the flight, we were told that, in the event there was a change in cabin pressure, oxygen masks would automatically fall from a compartment just above our heads. We were then instructed that if we were traveling with a small child or someone else needing assistance, we were "*to place the mask on yourself first* before attempting to assist another person."

Helping yourself before you help someone else may seem self-centered at first, but in order to really help someone, it's an essential first step.

Let's use our airplane scenario as an example. A loss in cabin pressure translates to a loss of oxygen. Lack of oxygen, or hypoxia, causes disorientation and impaired judgment, rendering its victim incapable of making a rational decision. In the event of an "explosive decompression" of the passenger cabin (meaning a sudden and rapid loss of cabin pressure) at a normal cruising altitude (of 29,000–35,000 feet), occupants have *less than five seconds* to don their oxygen masks before becoming completely unconscious.

Suppose this was the case, and you were attempting to help the person next to you without first attending to your own safety. And suppose that person struggled against your efforts, which is likely to be the case with a person who is suffering from panic and hypoxia. The extra time, energy, and effort you would expend would surely deplete the vital oxygen required for you to remain conscious, and you, too, would quickly become incapacitated. The result would be *two* people in grave danger.

The same scenario can be applied to all other situations in life. Not taking care of your basic needs, taking action from a position of weakness rather than strength, could have harmful consequences for both you and those you aim to help: *You can't give what you lack yourself.*

In order to perform at the optimal levels necessary to help rather than hurt, you must have, at all times, a surplus of physical, spiritual, mental, and financial energy. If we lack even one of these essential elements, we can't expect to develop the resources required to make a significant difference in anyone's life — including our own. There are very few guarantees in life. But one I'll give you is this: If you rush to serve others before you are prepared to, you'll fail. This is where our natural predisposition to selfishness — survival — can come to our aid. If we allow it to work properly, our natural survival instinct can tell us what we should or should not be doing in cases where our life is threatened. It's nature that keeps us from kicking over motorcycles belonging to a gang of drunken Hell's Angels, and it is nature that can cause us to turn away from helping others when we are in desperate need of help ourselves. But one of the deepest cravings of human nature is, according to William James, to be appreciated. Our desire for appreciation and acceptance can easily get in the path of both our natural survival instinct and sense of good judgment.

A conflict arises within us when we allow our natural desire for acceptance and appreciation to overpower our natural tendency for self-preservation — like when a good friend comes to us in need at a time when we are already up to our necks in commitments, and we yield to our desire to be a good friend and agree to lend time, energy, or money that we do not have. When we do this, we allow our desires, our *wants*, to get in the way of our *needs*. We allow ourselves to be driven by our desires because we are selfishly seeking a form of instant gratification: the satisfaction we get from being recognized as the kind of friend a person can count on. We should, however, be focused on what we need to do; we should prioritize our commitments, perhaps saying "no" now and again to ensure that we are physically, mentally, spiritually, and financially able to follow through on the select promises we do make without bankrupting our body, soul, and our children's college fund. We'll talk a lot more about the disparity between wants and needs as we progress in our work together, but for now it is important that you realize wants can get in the way of needs, and when they do, they surely trip us up.

The Sun Was Shining When Noah Built His Ark

Preparation is vital for success. When we turn to others for help, we naturally expect they will be prepared to give us their very best. We understand inherently that anything less can potentially cause us harm or, at the very least, diminish the results. The clash between wants and needs can occur at any moment, and when it does, it can impair the judgment of even the best trained and dedicated among us.

Weeks before her eighty-second birthday, my mother confronted a decision that, thanks to continuing advances in medicine, a growing number of people will face. Her aging heart was failing: the valves that control the flow of blood from one side of the heart to the other were calcified to the point they no longer worked. The discovery was made during a routine examination, at which point Mom was whisked away to a regional heart center and prepared for emergency surgery.

It was two o'clock in the morning by the time a surgeon came into her room to discuss the impending procedure with her. "You require a triple bypass and both valves in your heart need to be replaced," the surgeon said. "I estimate the procedure will take about ten hours to complete," he added matter-of-factly, "and I want to get it done right away."

Mom, who'd been a practicing, registered nurse for sixty years, understood the risks associated with such extensive surgery and the skill and judgment required of the surgeon.

"How long have you been on your feet today, Doctor?" Mom inquired.

"I've been operating since six o'clock yesterday morning. I guess that makes it about twenty-two hours," the young doctor replied.

Mom just smiled that little smile of hers and said, "The way I see it, Doctor, we have two options. You could yield to your sense of urgency and rush me down to the operating room now, or you could go home, get a good night's sleep, and we can attack this thing in the morning."

Before the doctor could even respond, Mom smiled again and said, "Pleasant dreams, Doctor."

Message delivered, message received. "I'll see you in the morning," he said, shaking his head as he walked from the room.

Part of the young doctor's essential preparation should have been to ensure that he had what he needed to perform the surgery, including enough rest to be able to function at his optimum. Mom was determined he get the rest he desperately needed, and it may have saved them both from a traumatic experience. Sometimes we need to be reminded of our own limitations. Judging when we are "low on fuel" seems most difficult for people who have a natural drive to serve — who almost instinctively jump to the aid of those in need — like the young doctor in the example. These people are so used to giving that it has become part of who they are. They possess a seemingly innate desire to help, coupled with a sense of urgency to do so. But if we yield to that desire and focus on what we want — which is to help anyone and everyone in need — we end up trying to give others what we lack, and the only reward we can expect for our efforts will be, at best, personal failure and, at worst, harm to the very people we hoped to help in the first place.

I'm harping on this issue for a reason. I've seen — and felt — the devastating outcome when a person who is in a compromised state jumps to the rescue of those in need.

Some time ago, I was acting as chief executive officer of a company I had founded eight years prior. The use of the word "acting" in the above sentence is not accidental. I was called back to run the company during the interim absence of a CEO. This might have worked, except I had been out of touch with the daily operations of that particular business for five years. I was not familiar with how much the needs of our organization and the industry in which it operated had changed. Additionally, I was spread far too thinly with prior obligations to devote the time, energy, and resources necessary to meet the full-time demands of a chief executive. What I should have done was suggest an alternative solution, or at least postpone my involvement until I had had time to prepare. But a call for help, especially from those you care most about, can make you lose sight of priorities.

I walked headstrong into a huge problem. Our company needed to revamp its entire computer system, which was growing more ineffective and costly each day. Data management is the lifeblood of a business organization. Interruptions in payroll, billing, credit, or collections can cause small organizations painful suffering, and large ones to drop to their knees. With a thousand or so employees, and many millions of dollars in play at any given moment, our organization fit better into the latter category.

I wanted to solve the problem as quickly as I could and return to my other obligations. I attended meetings at the end of already taxing days and made critical decisions when I was physically, mentally, and emotionally drained. At one of these meetings, I made the decision to entirely revamp our data-management system.

Based on my approval, the company entered into an agreement with a consulting firm to upgrade our computer hardware and software. This process involved the transfer of our vital company data from the old system to the new and the training of our key employees in the care and feeding of the new system.

I did not act with the proper diligence when examining the consulting firm's qualifications and capabilities, and, as it turned out, the firm lacked the proper knowledge, experience, time, and financial wherewithal to see the project through. They ended up going out of business before our project was completed — which, coincidently, was just about a week before the entire system crashed. The result was a disaster.

The entire data-management system was out of commission and our business was catapulted into the dark ages. I'm not even going to begin to explain what it was like to have to prepare over a thousand paychecks using a manual accounting system, with only two days' notice. It took months to get the system "live" again, and nine years (of overtime wages) to catch up with the resulting backlog.

In my haste to get things done, I caused enough harm to almost put an end to a highly profitable organization. I learned a very costly lesson during that trying period: *You can't sell from an empty cart.* You simply can't give what you are physically, mentally, spiritually, or financially unable to give.

So, what's the solution? Preparation, doing first things first. In order to be successful at what we *want* to do, we must first do what we *need* to do: Prepare ourselves to serve. We need to begin preparing ourselves now for what we will be called upon to do in the future.

Fill Your Cart before You Head to Market

In this section of *Never Offer Your Comb to a Bald Man*, we will go about the task of developing a surplus of physical, mental, spiritual, and financial resources in you. You can then draw from these resources to effectively serve the needs of others.

CHAPTER 6

I've Fallen and I Can't Get Up!

The most obvious dimension of our *whole self* can be said to be our physical body, the living, breathing, blood-pumping part of us that is our substantive form.

From a "trade-in" value, at least, our physical bodies are virtually worthless. Consisting mostly of water and a few petty weights of trace minerals — even the most beautiful among us, if we were reduced to our basic parts, wouldn't command more than a dollar and seventy-three cents in scrap value. Face it; from the neck down, we're little more than hairy masses of flesh, skin, and bones, capable of performing only the most basic of life-sustaining tasks.

All I've just said is not meant, however, to imply we can neglect our physical bodies — quite the contrary. Ask anyone who's ever lost *good physical health*, even for a brief period, and they will tell you that it is invaluable. Without our physical health, nothing else seems to matter much.

A healthy physical body enables us to do many of the things we take for granted, such as care for ourselves, move from place to place, fend off attackers, and perpetuate our species. A healthy physical body also enhances our lives by allowing us to enjoy the physical pleasure and intimacy of one another. It allows us to express our sexuality and physical love for another person. Besides all of the physical tasks our bodies help us accomplish, they also make an excellent and convenient resting place for our brains.

Like any other piece of machinery, if we neglect caring for and maintaining our physical bodies, they break down. And when our bodies break down, our very existence is left open to question. Perhaps that's why nature plays such an important part in reminding us to care for our basic physical needs. We get hungry and thirsty at regular intervals — as reminders to nourish and hydrate our bodies. When darkness falls, our pineal gland secretes the hormone melatonin, triggering our bodies to fall asleep and so insuring our need for physical rest is met. We shiver and sweat to control our body temperature; and most of us, at least, tend to yield to our natural sense of fear, which instinctively keeps us from pulling the tail of an irritable tiger or shouting the phrase "yeah, so sue me!" at an out-of-work lawyer.

Nature sends out signals for the proper care, feeding, and maintenance of the human machine. The problem comes when we work against nature by turning our back on the signals. A young, ambitious, yet not-so-bright entrepreneur I once knew — okay, I confess, it was me — learned a valuable lesson some time ago, about the need for proper care and preventative maintenance with respect to his human machine.

I started my first business venture with the same zeal any healthy, hungry, motivated, newly self-employed twenty-six-year-old would have. I worked all day, peddling the services of my burgeoning business to prospective clients, and then spent all evening performing those services.

Nights and weekends were simply the time allotted for paperwork, bookkeeping and tax preparation, marketing and advertising, typing contract proposals, filing, banking, and all the rest of the fun tasks associated with running a small business.

As the business grew, so did my lack of free time. My daily routine evolved into one, seemingly uninterrupted, blur. Each day I would arise before the sun, to get a jump on the business of the day, and I would proceed at a nonstop pace until well after midnight. After three or so hours of restless sleep, I'd begin anew.

My only form of physical exercise was worrying. As a consequence, I was severely out of shape: my waistline seemed to grow faster than my business.

I did, however, eat a balanced diet, consisting of all the major food groups — ice cream, candy bars, caffeine, and nicotine. As busy as my schedule got, I nevertheless did make a point of eating one complete meal at least once a week — a chili dog and a Coke.

As for rest and recuperation, who had the time? I rarely, if ever, took time off. If I wasn't conducting business, I was talking about conducting business, thinking about conducting business, or dreaming about conducting business.

Vacations were also out of the question. I was too busy trying to meet an ever-growing, weekly payroll to concern myself with taking time off. I stopped making time for friends and family, too. People became so tired of inviting me to functions, only to hear the same old excuse of being too busy, they eventually stopped calling.

I stopped meditating and praying, and I even stopped keeping my journal, a practice I had maintained since I was about twenty years old. And so it went for the next seven years. Then, one snowy February morning, nature sent me a wake-up call.

The day started out like any other: up at dawn, a hot cup of coffee for breakfast, then into the shower. That's where the familiar ended.

As my wife tells it, "all I heard was the shower running and then an awful thud." The thud was me, collapsing on the shower floor — and she was right, it was awful.

A prolonged lack of attention had weakened my immune system enough to allow the invasion of a renegade, drug-resistant strain of pneumonia to enter my lungs. As I lay in the hospital bed, watching the news account of the death of Muppets creator Jim Henson, who had just succumbed to the same brand of pneumonia I was wrestling with, I vowed to begin taking better care of my health.

Since that day, I have learned to schedule time for myself. I carve out at least an hour each day for physical exercise. I take routine breaks throughout the day to walk and stretch. I've learned to eat sensibly, and in an unhurried manner. I take daily vitamin supplements and undergo regular checkups. I take a few days off each month and at least three extended holidays each year to recharge my batteries. I've also learned to say "no" to a great number of "opportunities."

What has been the result of all this slothful behavior? My productivity has increased tenfold. Today I'm getting more accomplished than I ever did in those early years. I oversee the running of a number of very successful business ventures, speak to groups all over the country, promote, produce, and perform executive leadership retreats, consult various business, governmental, and association leaders, write books and articles, and even find an odd moment or two to work as a professional voice-over artist.

Defining the Ultimate Goal for Our Physical Self

If we lack a high abundance of physical energy, stamina, and strength, we will be of little use to anyone. If we are to be effec-

tive at serving the needs of others, we must serve our own physical needs first and forever.

So, what would be the ultimate goal for the physical self?
Would it be immortality? Well, in order for a goal to be an
effective motivator, it must be both beneficial to our welfare and
attainable, and since no one can live forever, immortality can't
be a goal for you and me to shoot for. What might we use in its
place?

Suppose, instead of immortality, we make *wellness* our ultimate physical goal? The goal of *wellness* makes sense from a
practical, servant-leadership standpoint: The longer we can
keep ourselves living healthily, the longer we will be able to
serve the needs of others and the greater our expected rewards
will be.

Wellness is not purely about physical health; it's also about
sound mental, spiritual, and financial health; the four are
inexorably connected and must be in balance for any type of
abundance to exist and flourish. A person's mental state, sense
of connectedness to others, and financial state can have a large
role in his or her overall quality of life. These factors can have
either a positive or deleterious effect on physical health, and for
this reason, we need to address all areas of the self before calling our wellness plan complete. Later chapters will go further
into the concepts of financial, spiritual, and mental wellness.
We'll start with the easy one, physical wellness.

Your Personal Wellness Plan for Physical Health

To make sure I would give you the best advice I could, I
enlisted the help of some of the top wellness physicians in the
country. What follows is a distillation of their cumulative
advice. The doctors I have spoken to assure me that by import-
ing as many of these simple tips as practicable into your daily

regimen, you can greatly enhance the quality and possibly the quantity of your life — save, of course, a stray bullet, a pandemic, a high-speed encounter with a stationary object, or a fall in the bathtub.

Step #1: Adjust Your Attitude. When it comes to matters of health care, in our pharmaceutically dominant Western culture, most of us have been conditioned to view our health from the perspective of preventing illness rather than supporting wellness.

We go about our daily lives rarely giving thought to the condition of our health, until something goes wrong. In this sense, we live our lives like we drive our cars. Although we drive our cars with regularity, we tend to pay very little attention to, for example, the gauges located on the dashboard; these gauges are designed to allow us to monitor strategic systems in the car, like the brakes, engine temperature, battery function, and the like. Most of us drive our cars without giving these systems or the gauges a second thought — that is, until something goes wrong. Often we take the same hands-off attitude to living: ignoring our body's vital gauges — pain, fatigue, irritability, et cetera — that can signal that something is amiss. We simply drive our bodies until something goes wrong. Only then do we run to the mechanic . . . ugh, I mean doctor, and seek her advice.

The first step, then, in attaining your goal of physical wellness is changing your attitude about health from one of *illness* to one of *wellness*. Once your attitude has been properly screwed on and is facing in the right direction, you can walk yourself through the following steps toward a life of wellness.

Step #2: Start with a Good Physical Examination. If you have never had a complete physical examination or haven't had one in some time, get one. Just make sure the person giving you the examination is capable of not only assessing your present health but also advising you about how to achieve your goal of wellness. Seek a doctor who has a philosophy that is committed to wellness. There are many capable wellness-oriented physicians in close proximity to your home; you may simply have to ferret them out from the rest.

To find a good wellness practitioner, Henri Roca, M.D., founder and president of the Wholistic Wellness Network and himself a wellness expert, suggests the following: First, make sure that the practitioner is well trained and effective. If the person claims to have a certification, ask to see it. Then ask specific questions about the training required for that certification. Get a sense for how you connect with the practitioner. You must trust your practitioner in order for his or her suggestions to be effective. If you feel uncomfortable in any way, then it's time to look for another practitioner.

Finally, remember this person can't do it for you. Change requires that you make an effort, and you have to be willing to be directed. If the practitioner says you don't have to work at changing your lifestyle, beware: I have never seen a lifestyle transformation that did not require effort.

Step #3: Develop a Personal Wellness Team. You are going to find a plethora of qualified, highly skilled professionals ready, willing, and able to help you in achieving your wellness goal. However, you may have to adjust your attitude with respect to the part your doctor and other health-care professionals play in your life. You need to look at your doctor, physical therapist, nutritionist, personal trainer, and other wellness advisers as guides rather than as fix-it men and women. Once you have selected the wellness team you feel is best for you, be open with the members of your team: tell each what your ultimate goal is and enlist his or her advice and support in meeting your objectives.

Step #4: Develop a Personal Wellness Plan. The purpose of

recruiting a team of experts is to develop an integrated, personal wellness plan — designed specifically for you.

What should your plan include? Well, the answers are as varied and unique as the number of people on earth; however, two areas experts agree should always be addressed are exercise and diet.

Concerning the first, once you and your doctor have determined your physical ability, get off the couch and out from behind the keyboard and do something! To stay physically fit you gotta move. Get involved in some type of activity that will raise your heart rate to a high, but safe, level (known as your target heart rate) for at least twenty minutes. Jogging, cross-country skiing, swimming, even brisk walking or a little pickup basketball will work.

Changing rituals in your daily routine also helps. For instance, take a walk for lunch instead of eating the high-fat meal you had planned; take the stairs instead of the elevator; park at the furthest spot in the parking lot, not the closest one to the door, as you usually do. Physical fitness has more to do with *flexibility* than with physical strength, and this becomes more apparent as we age. Many doctors I have consulted tell me that most of the quality-of-life issues they deal with result from a lifestyle of inactivity that leads to lack of joint mobility and flexibility. An excellent prophylactic for these maladies is an exercise modality that promotes flexibility, like yoga.

In the area of diet, you should work with a qualified nutritional counselor to develop a diet that is specific to your own particular needs and toward a goal of optimum health.

Step #5: Stick to Your Plan. From this point on, success is up to you. Nobody can force you to follow your plan; you must want to achieve the result you are after and be willing to change your behavior in order to get there. Changing your behavior may be hard work, but as Dr. Kenneth Cooper, a noted wellness physician, advises: "It's easier to maintain good health than to regain it once it's lost."

Dr. Roca adds: "Abundance is a mind state. It acknowledges one has all one needs in order to accomplish all of one's goals and more. Applied to wellness and physical energy, abundance applies to those who are in a state of wellness and are physically fit, have greater levels of energy, and can accomplish acts requiring strength and stamina with ease.

"For those of us who are not quite so fit, we can fake it till we make it. We can create a frame of mind that allows us to believe that we have an abundance of physical energy. With every piece of exercise we do, with every modicum of fitness we achieve, our energy level and our state of wellness increases."

CHAPTER 7

The Care and Feeding of the Mental Self

Just as we need to maintain a reservoir of physical stamina to effectively serve the needs of others, we must also maintain an abundant surplus of mental power. We need to acquire and cultivate a broad, continually expanding base of knowledge in order to meet the changing situations ahead.

I once heard a fellow comment, "I've already got my degree, so I don't see any need to waste my time learning anything else." What a pity, I thought. Here's an intelligent, reasonably successful guy who's about to get blindsided by the steamroller of change.

Whether we like it or not, the universe and all its parts are changing. To think that we can somehow meet tomorrow's needs with today's outdated solutions is farcical. If we don't change along with the rest of the universe, we're headed straight for obscurity.

Many of the challenges we face today couldn't have been conceived of five short years ago. In 1996, you could count on the fingers of one hand the number of people who even knew what the Internet was, now what were once greasy-spoon coffee shops have become cyber cafés; the term "cyber crime" has been coined, and issues surrounding it are baffling law-enforcement agencies around the world. Even the neighbor-hood pizza shop has joined the cyber flock, printing its Web site address on the lid of pizza boxes, right next to the phrase "You've tried the rest, now try the best."

Future challenges will look nothing like those we face today. If your base of knowledge isn't constantly expanding, you don't stand a chance against what's waiting for you around the next corner. But this is only part of the problem.

From a more basic standpoint, the human mind is designed to continually learn new things. To operate most effectively, the mind needs to be constantly challenged and exposed to new stimuli.

A lack of intellectual stimulation can have some very unpleasant outcomes with respect to our physical, mental, spiritual, and financial health. We've gotta keep learning new and different things in order to keep our minds, bodies, spirits, and finances healthy.

Intellectual laziness can cause a human being to become apathetic and self-focused. Experts say apathy and self-centeredness often lead to anxiety and depression, hypochondria, insomnia, and a host of other neurotic behaviors.

Chances are, when we live under these negative conditions long enough, we will soon experience a lack of abundance in other aspects of our lives. I know personally how grievous an apathetic, self-focused attitude can be: during the times in my life when I was emotionally bankrupt, I was also physically, spiritually, and financially bankrupt.

With some exceptions, the propensity toward intellectual laziness begins taking hold in our early thirties, when the majority of us are finished with our formal education. The older we get, the worse the problem tends to become.

I live and work not far from one of the largest concentrations of retirement complexes in the northeastern United States, and I have seen firsthand what happens to many people when they quit working. In no time at all, once-vibrant, productive, good-natured individuals are reduced to a wild band of mind-numbed, early-bird-dining, chronically complaining, hypochondriacal curmudgeons, intent on letting you know "how miserable it is to get old."

Conversely, I have seen what happens to people who continue to learn new things, take on new and exciting challenges, and live their lives to the fullest, often pursuing a job or profession they love right up until the day they die. Take my friend Pete, for instance. Pete retired from a successful business, but didn't retire from working.

A CPA with forty-plus years of accounting experience, Pete began an intensive study of the specialized needs of not-for-profit organizations the day he announced he was leaving his lucrative accounting firm. For the past ten years Pete has been busier than ever, giving his services away. He now serves, free of charge, his church, a local hospital, and a number of other organizations he has "adopted," by providing them with new and innovative management and tax strategies. When we stop learning and keeping up with the changes in the world around us, we lose our ability to be as effective as we could be. When this happens, we choke out any hope of identifying and meeting the needs of others, thus limiting our own returns in the process.

Open Your Mind

Just as we need an ultimate goal with respect to our physical selves, we must have one for the development of our mental selves, and it is *lifelong learning.*

Why is *lifelong learning* such a necessary mental goal? In order to be most effective, the learning we undertake must be as broad-based as possible and as vast as life itself, and this requires a lifelong effort. The greater and more diverse your scope of knowledge, the better outfitted you will be to meet the evolving needs of others.

The role of a servant leader is unlike that of any other. The best analogy I have heard to describe the spirit of servant leadership is that of the potter and the clay. To be servant leaders, we must be as malleable as the clay in the potter's hands; the clay must yield to the potter's intention.

Force yourself to develop an open mind. My friend Zig Ziglar says: "Most people's minds are like concrete . . . all mixed-up and permanently set." We tend to adopt a particular way of thinking and then hold onto it as if it were made of diamonds. Servant leaders need to maintain an open mind with respect to all things and all people. I'm not suggesting you need to subscribe to a new set of values or beliefs; I'm simply saying you need to learn to appreciate the point of view of another. We need to learn to agree to disagree and still maintain our inseparable connection with all of humanity. Just because I don't agree with you on a particular issue doesn't mean I can't learn from you or serve your needs.

Read and experience things outside of your comfort zone. If you've labeled yourself politically conservative, you should subscribe to at least one publication that is written from a radically liberal point of view. I make it a point to buy and read one magazine and one book each month from a list of topics I find particularly offensive. I admit I still look around a bit to make sure no one I know sees me buying the stuff — I didn't say I was comfortable reading it, I just read it. Another way to accomplish this is to attend a meeting or join an organization that has opinions differing from the ones you hold dearest to your heart.

Seek out acquaintances and associations with people who are markedly different from you. I like this one a lot. The immortal words of Groucho Marx, about never joining a club that would allow him in as a member, serve as a reminder: If we only associate with people who are accepting of us and who share our views and experience, we will never grow past the point of our present experience.

If we are to become effective as servant leaders, we must be willing to become what those we serve need us to be. To accomplish this, we need to be knowledgeable about a great number of subjects. We need to expand the scope of our understanding of people and the reasons they do the things they do. We need to acquire knowledge, even in areas where we have no interest or little comfort. Remember, serving others is about responding to *their* needs, not to our own.

We can make ourselves able to accomplish this seemingly impossible task simply by expanding our depth of knowledge in the following three key areas:

Self-knowledge: You need to learn more about yourself, your capabilities, and your limitations: how to identify and develop your natural talents and uncover your hidden ones. You need to learn more about what causes your fears, doubts, and worries, and how to eliminate them from your life. You need to learn to mine the gems of knowledge hidden in every experience of your life — the good, the bad, and the ugly.

Knowledge of Others: Once you gain a better insight into yourself, then you can concentrate your efforts on learning what you need to know about others. You need to gain better insight into others and learn how to identify their needs, both the apparent ones and — most valuable of all — those that lie below the surface.

Acquiring Universal Knowledge: You need to learn to change your attitude about where your knowledge comes from. You must seek to learn something from everyone you meet, no matter how humble their occupation or position in life, or how different or even offensive their ideas are compared to yours.

Getting to Know You

In part 3 of *Never Offer Your Comb to a Bald Man*, we'll cover what you need to learn about the behavior and tendencies of others and about the world in which we live. But first, you need to become even more familiar with something a little bit closer to home — yourself.

In the first century A.D., Socrates wrote: "The life which is unexamined is not worth living." The Greek words "know thyself" were inscribed in twenty-four karat gold on the wall of the temple of Delphi. It was believed that the wisdom of these words was too great to have come from a mortal and so must have descended from Apollo himself.

The advice "know thyself" recurs throughout recorded history and is undoubtedly sound advice. Why then have so few people over the centuries heeded this counsel? Perhaps the answer to this fundamental question lies in the words of the philosopher Thales, who said, "For man to know himself is the hardest thing in the world."

Self-examination is undeniably difficult; it involves deep thinking and the willingness to take a close, sometimes painful, look at ourselves and our actions toward our fellows. The process of self-examination may uncover things about your character that you find disturbing or hard to admit — even to yourself; it might be a long and difficult process, but it is worth every bit of effort. In it, we learn to uncover our legitimate self.

You may, perhaps for the first time in your life, be forced to examine your motives, decisions, choices, and values. Self-examination may even require you to change — which, perhaps, is the single greatest reason most people never make the attempt.

We tend to go through life with three distinct and different images of who we are. In one image, we see ourselves as we think we are; in another, we see ourselves as we believe others see us; and in the third, we see the real person, the same person God sees.

Each of us has within us a legitimate self and an illusory self. We keep the legitimate self hidden behind a veil of self-deception, misconceived frailties, false humility, and cleverly constructed masks that hide our true feelings of defenselessness. Just as our reflection in a mirror is an illusion of our real self, the person we often present to others is only a reflection, a superficial image of the person we really are inside. Most of us have played this part so long that the image we see of ourselves is an indistinguishable blur from the substance of our legitimate self. When this happens, we must rediscover the person we truly are, which is actually far easier than it sounds.

Our legitimate self, unlike the illusion we often portray to others, has substance. Self-examination is like a refracting lens, sharpening the edges and helping us distinguish between the two images we hold of ourselves. It also helps us to scrutinize our motives, choices, and the real reasons behind the good deeds we hold up for all to see.

Once you rid yourself of the enervating burdens of the past and illusions that have worked to shroud the real you, you will, perhaps for the first time, be able to take a clear, honest look at yourself as you really are, not as you wish you were, nor as others have led you to believe you are. In this new light of truth, you will discover, accept, and appreciate the real person that lives inside you, and you will gain an incalculable degree of personal power in the process.

You Don't Have to Be Perfect to Live a Purposeful Life

Journaling and using other self-discovery tools are undoubtedly going to help you learn more about yourself, your talents, and abilities, as well as how and why you do the things you do. But before you can even begin applying any of this new-found knowledge, there is a little attitude adjustment you may have to make. If you're still breathing, chances are you have a definite attitude living deep inside you with regard to making mistakes. There seems to be something in the human makeup that causes us to feel less of ourselves when we stumble and fall, when we realize that we are not perfect.

I'm not sure where the above idea originated. Perhaps it was passed down to us from the Garden of Eden or the monkeys in the jungle — depending upon where your personal theories of origin lie. Maybe it's the result of a school system that trained its teachers in such a way they inadvertently overlooked our successes while they chastised us for our mistakes. It might be the effects of a religious system that sets standards of morality beyond the reach of most mortals. Or, maybe it's just the fact that we have simply misunderstood the message.

Whatever the cause, the result is the same: we tend to be too hard on ourselves. Most, if not all, of us are our own worst critics. And the simple fact is that we come dangerously close to self-destruction when we make "perfection" our goal.

In the mid-fifteenth century, philosopher Nicholas of Cusa wrote a three volume treatise entitled *On Learned Ignorance*. The main theme of his work centered on man's futile search for absolute knowledge. In the first volume, Nicholas explains that humans have a natural desire for knowledge but become frustrated when they realize the enduring fact of their own ignorance. The only solution, Nicholas concludes, is for people to seek their own ignorance. Centuries before, Socrates advised: "If a man makes his own ignorance the object of his desire for knowledge, he can acquire a learned ignorance."

The suggestion here is that, by reflecting on his own limitations, man can, to some extent, surmount his own ignorance. The moment we realize that the quiddity of things, their absolute "whatness," is beyond our ken, is the very moment we draw closer to the truth that we have been seeking all along. In this sense, the search for absolute knowledge is like our quest for personal perfection — futile.

We will never be perfect. I know for some of you this comes as a bit of bad news. If it does, here's the good news: perfection is not, as many of us have been unwittingly led to believe, a necessary element in the alchemy of a fulfilling and meaningful life, nor is it a prerequisite for success in any endeavor.

We can foster a healthier attitude with respect to our quest for perfection by hitchhiking on Nicholas's conclusion regarding the human search for ultimate knowledge. We can opt to strive for self-betterment, with the understanding that absolute perfection is unattainable, knowing that our best efforts are enough to succeed. This is a much more beneficial life goal.

Self-improvement is certainly a worthy goal. But if in the process we become so hard on ourselves that we stifle the very growth we seek, we only end up causing ourselves to feel unworthy of success. So, when we are engaged in the process of self-improvement, we need to be careful who we listen to — including ourselves.

The first step in self-improvement is learning to be kind to yourself, knowing that you are *good enough*, even if you will never be perfect. And, you don't have to be perfect to live a purposeful life as a servant leader.

The following suggestions can help you begin the delicate and time-consuming process of self-discovery. If you vow to continue the process for the rest of your life, I can promise you this: you will gain from the experience an entirely new and positive view of yourself and your role in the universe. At the very least, you will catch a glimpse of the person who is living in the shadows of your life, and who knows, you may just like what you see.

Discovering the Real You

Who are you — really? What personal characteristics, unique life experiences, natural talents, physical attributes separate you from the pack? What is it about you that enables you to see things differently from those around you? Why do you behave in the way you do? Why is it easy to relate to some people you meet and almost impossible to connect with others?

Have you ever put any serious thought to the above questions? Have you ever sat down and taken an accurate inventory of the unique qualities, traits, feelings, thoughts, emotions, and points of view that comprise the miracle that is living inside you? If you answered "no" to that last question, you're not alone. The fact is, most people are far too busy deciding who they *aren't*, rather than who they are, wishing they had that guy's looks or that woman's talent.

It's unfortunate, really, how we tend to define our personal successes by weighing them against the successes of others, rather than how we should: by comparing *what we have accomplished*, given our own set of unique skills, talents, experiences, and abilities, with *what we might not have accomplished*. The only gain from comparing our achievements with others' is purely negative: a diminished sense of worth from constant self-flagellation and an untold host of missed opportunities, thinking we can only accomplish things with someone else's talents, characteristics, and resources.

If we spent half as much time identifying and strengthening our own natural resources as we did in wishing we possessed those of another, there would be no telling what we might be capable of. But, life has proven we will rarely change our point of reference without making a conscious effort to do so. So, this is the first thing you must do in order to prepare yourself to better serve the needs of others.

To accomplish this task, I'll give you an idea of some of the tools others have used to aid in self-discovery. You can use any or all of the techniques outlined in this chapter, or perhaps you may discover a few of your own. A successful outcome in the self-discovery exercise seems to have less to do with the specific tools you employ and more with the fact that you are actually doing the exercise. I believe the exercise of self-examination is the thing that holds the magic, rather than the specific methods used to achieve those ends. Having said this, there is one tool that, for the purposes of our work here, is indispensable — a personal journal.

Fourteen Minutes a Day to a More Meaningful Life

Do you keep a journal? You should. A journal can give you a better understanding of your life. It can reveal what you choose to invest your time in each day and why. It can reveal things about the patterns in your life — both constructive and destructive — that you would have otherwise missed.

Like a candle in the darkness, your journal can illuminate hidden patterns in your life, some of which may be standing in your way of success. A journal is also your biography, a personal and permanent chronicle of your struggles and successes over them.

A journal can help you to acknowledge problems in your life, sometimes before they even arise. The act of writing your problems out causes you to look at them objectively. It provides you with a point of reference, allowing you to view the events that might have precipitated them. By documenting life's troubling events in your journal, you are better able to view your problems in the light of objectivity and see what effect they are having on your attitudes and actions.

Thinking about your life and its events is not the same as writing about it. The act of writing in your journal brings together both sides of your brain — your creative side and your judicial side. It also helps to clear your mind. Writing down your problems helps the brain transfer them from your subconscious to your conscious mind, taking them off the already overloaded mental "back burner."

Journaling also yields a cumulative benefit: It will help you to see your life as it unfolds, matching your challenges with your actions and your actions with your outcomes. Since you are recording your experiences as they actually happen, you soon find that you are able to accumulate a recognizable, tangible, and factual record of your personal growth. This helps you see the progress you have made, especially during those more difficult times, when you feel that you are *no further ahead now than you were ten years ago*. Through continued daily journaling, you will actually begin to see that your life is going somewhere.

Without a written documentation of events, the details of the day blend together in an indistinguishable blur. It's easy to become blind to life's subtle directional shifts. When we do, we end up assuming the role of a passive spectator in our own lives, seemingly uninvolved in the events that shape our destiny. In actuality, nothing could be further from the truth.

Journaling may even help you to discover within yourself a talent, ability, or resources that you did not know previously existed.

If you have never kept a journal, you may not know how or where to begin. If this is the case, I have outlined below the method I have used for the past twenty-five years. I don't do anything very elaborate; I just keep a regular log of the events, feelings, and emotions that shape my life — with an occasional graph, sketch, or diagram.

I've provided the following outline *only as an example.* Remember this is *your* journal, not mine; use the method of record keeping that you find works best for you.

The first thing you will need is something to write in. In the beginning, I used a spiral notebook. Today I use a hardbound writing journal; I alternate between lined and unlined, having no preference for either. I do, however, always use a fountain pen, simply because I enjoy the *feel* of writing with a fine writing instrument. You can achieve the same results with a chewed up number two pencil and a coffee stained, yellow legal pad.

The next thing you will need to do is to schedule time for your journal entries. The best time for this is either just before you retire or first thing upon rising.

Writing in your journal just before you go to sleep does have one distinct advantage: it helps you sleep better. Writing down your thoughts lessens the clutter in your mind and allows you to sleep.

Over the years, I've discovered a second benefit to writing in the evening. You are able to recapitulate and document the events of the day while they are fresh in your mind. The longer you wait, of course, the duller the memory becomes. This is not to say that I don't, from time to time, make records in my journal when I wake in the morning, because I frequently do. I've even been known to get out of bed in the middle of the night and begin writing, especially during particularly stressful or emotionally troubling times. I have even paused to record an event that has a specific significance in my life as it is happening or shortly after.

Many folks I know use a more "current event driven" style, making frequent notations in their journal through the day. You can utilize a daily planner like those marketed by Daytimer, Franklin Planner, or various other stationery houses that provide a page-a-day format. The page-a-day format is important because it provides you sufficient writing space to record the day's events in real time. The obvious benefit to this method is it helps you to record the details of an event while they are fresh in your mind, before your subconscious has had a chance to embellish or otherwise distort them.

Even though you may opt to use one journaling technique — recapitulation — over the other as your primary journaling style, don't be afraid to flip-flop between styles as you go; in fact, it can be quite helpful. You may, for example, want to record a particularly significant event as it happens, especially if it happens to provoke a profound emotional response in you.

Before you begin writing the events of day one in your journal, you need to prepare your mind for the exercise. The best way to do that is to sit in a comfortable position, in a quiet place where you will not be disturbed. Simply sit quietly — close your eyes if you'd like — and let your mind wander.

Since you will never be able to make your mind go completely blank, don't even try. Just give way to your mental wandering. Allow your mind to jump from thought to thought without resistance.

After a few moments of sitting quietly, you will begin to feel a certain rhythm to your natural breathing. Become tuned to your natural rhythms and feel them synchronize to the natural cadence of life. Not only will this practice help you to relax and organize your thoughts better, it will also help you to get in tune with your life and your surroundings, to slow the pace of your life to a manageable one, something we'll speak more of in an upcoming chapter.

Once you have spent some time in the silence, begin to reflect on the events of the day. Play the day's events over in your mind, like a movie, tracing your steps in as much detail as possible; try to mentally relive the events, actions, emotions, successes and failures, wishes and hopes, that comprise the most recent segment of your life's journey.

What you record and how you record it is up to you. A journal is personal and should reflect your life and your personality, but here are a few questions that might serve to spark some creative ideas that will enhance your journal keeping; some are ones I have used personally, others I've collected over the years from fellow sojourners.

- When you woke this morning, were you in a pleasant mood or were you jarred from a deep sleep?
- Did you dream? Do you remember your dream? How did the events of your dreams make you feel?
- What was your energy level throughout the day? Why?
- What were the emotions, desires, plans, fears, and challenges that greeted you as you went about your day?
- As the day progressed, what changes did you experience in mood, emotions, physical energy level or other bodily changes?
- What was your mood like as you approached the tasks of the day? Can you connect anything about your mood to the eventual outcome of the task(s)?
- What types of emotions came up during the day?

- What type of relationships did you foster during the day?
- What were the opportunities that presented themselves to you today? How did you respond?
- What were the specifics of your interpersonal relations?
- What were your goals for the day? Did you accomplish what you set out to?

In a speech, television talk show host Oprah Winfrey gave this advice: "Keep a grateful journal. Every night, list five things that happened this day that you are grateful for. What it will begin to do is change your perspective of your day and your life. If you learn to focus on what you have, you will always see that the universe is abundant; you will have more. If you concentrate on what you don't have, you will never have enough." Certainly good advice, from someone who knows. Oprah has kept a journal for most of her life.

It's not surprising, then, to learn that in my dealings with successful servant leaders, I have not yet met one who has not, at one time or other, made journaling part of their life. I would go one step further and say that the very success they enjoy is rooted in the daily act of journaling.

Feel the Rhythm!

You should also try, as best as you can, to get a feel for the pace at which you are living your life, the rhythm of the day. The rhythm I speak of here is what I like to call "life rhythm," the natural rhythm that takes place deep inside you and all around you. The effects of these life rhythms, or "biorhythms," are not found on the surface of our actions; they take place on a deeper level: subtle changes in emotions and mood, such as when you feel as if you're speeding through life or that life is somehow passing you by.

When you have finished recording your recapitulation of

82

the day's events, go over the events of the day one more time and see what actions or events are connected with one another. When you finish analyzing your day, sit quietly once again in the calm, for just a few moments.

Faithfully repeat this practice every day of your life and you will see remarkable results. The time you spend — on average about fourteen minutes a day — will pay you back a thousandfold.

Learn to Identify, Embrace, and Celebrate Your Uniqueness

There really is no other person quite the same as you. No one with the same abilities, talents, dreams, personality, desires, hopes, and wishes. Even identical twins do not possess the same fundamental desires, dreams, or even personality.

With all the recent clamor and controversy surrounding the development of cloning and whether it is possible for science to clone a human being, a simple fact will always remain constant: Science will never be able to duplicate the thing that makes us as special as we are, the spirit — the soul. And it is the soul of the person that is the true and everlasting being.

The first step in celebrating you uniqueness is understanding that you are a special creature whose life has a special purpose. The next step is to learn everything there is to know about yourself and accept every part of you — unconditionally. The next step in tapping our mental powers is learning to uncover the secret riches and wonders that fate has written between the lines of our life story. This is where we are headed in the next chapter.

CHAPTER 8

The Good, the Bad, and the Ugly

L ife is full of experiences, some good, some not so good, and some that are so nasty we keep them hidden away from ourselves and from others. For most of us, our good experiences tend to serve as a symbol of the wonders and joys of life. Many of us have also learned how to allow the magic of the passage of time to soften the disappointing experiences in our lives to the point where we can reframe them in their proper perspective, affording us a rare opportunity to catch a glimmer of the hidden gifts that experience held for us. Some have even been able to courageously expose a segment of their lives they embarrassingly kept hidden from the world, and in doing so discovered one of their greatest gifts buried among the flotsam of shame, pain, and humiliation.

A colleague of mine, a woman I've always considered brilliant, once confessed a long-held secret fear of public ridicule for being thought of as "stupid." She recounted an event that took place when she was a child. Having apparently misunderstood her teacher's instructions for a routine homework assignment, my friend worked all weekend to complete what turned out to be the wrong project. The following Monday, the teacher, for whatever reason, publicly admonished the young pupil for her error. Since that day, my friend has harbored this memory and it has caused her to study every aspect of a situation and acquire a broad base of knowledge. She habitually checks and rechecks facts, never yielding to her assumptions. Her secret fear has worked to make her one of the finest business negotiators I have ever met, but the effect on her inner beliefs is more troubling: No matter how many successes she has in business or in life, she continues to feel less adequate than those around her.

Many of us travel through wonderful experiences without ever taking the chance to enjoy them. We allow the simple pleasures of life to slip through the cracks, forgetting the simple truth: Life is an adventure, not a destination.

I recently re-read the poem *Ithaca*, written by the Greek poet Constantine Cavafy. It reminded me that it is the voyage — the adventure on the way — that matters most, not the destination.

I had another reminder of this just the other day as I sat in the airport awaiting the departure of my flight from Philadelphia to Orlando. I watched a father of three, his wife trailing twenty steps behind, screech to a halt at the end of a long line that began at the check-in desk.

Turning to his baggage-laden wife, he bellowed, "Will you hurry up, you're going to make me miss the plane!" — a bit of an exaggeration, since the plane was not scheduled to begin boarding for at least another twenty minutes. I glanced over at his children, two boys and a girl, all about a year or so apart in age.

The little girl was about four years old and looked like a model for a Precious Moments doll — beautiful long strawberry-blond hair and sparkling blue eyes. Obviously tired from the jog from the parking lot, she hugged her father's leg and asked in a soft sigh, "Daddy, could you carry me?"

Her request went entirely unacknowledged. Assuming her father had not heard her the first time, she repeated her request. Only this time she raised her voice and colored it with a tinge of frustration, further making her point by emphasizing every syllable with a tug on his trouser leg: "Dad-dy-could-you-car-ry-me?"

Now, *that* got his attention. "Not now!" he barked. "Can't you see we're in a hurry?"

Meanwhile, the two boys were busy being — well, being boys — blissfully zooming around the lobby in their pretend airplanes, arms spread out like wings, jet sounds emanating from their mouths, imitating the airport scenes just outside the window.

The younger of the two, a cute kid with bright red hair, a gazillion freckles, and a missing front tooth, crash-landed into a nearby trash receptacle. This once again drew the attention of "Mr. Sweetness and Joy," who, through clenched teeth, hissed, "Will you two idiots grow up. This is no place to play, can't you see we're in a hurry?"

My glance was distracted by another scene. A couple, who looked to be in their mid-seventies, sat nearby, holding hands and leafing through what appeared to be a travel pamphlet outlining sights of interest at their intended destination. I was amused because they were apparently headed for Disney World. They laughed and smiled and gazed at each other with looks of quiet adoration.

I thought it funny that here, in the same 4,000-square-foot plot of earth, a person could view, simultaneously, both sides of the coin of life. On one side are people rushing their way through life, and on the other, those who are enjoying the adventure of the voyage.

I glanced back at the father of three, who was still standing in line at the check-in desk — jaw clenched, eyes firmly fixed on the front of the line, his right foot tapping out the rhythm of a man destined for a nervous breakdown, hypertension, or coronary thrombosis. This unhappy fellow was most likely in his mid-twenties, but the constipated expression on his face made him appear much older. The older couple, in contrast, shined with youthfulness.

Where we are headed in life is not nearly as important as how we get there. The construction of a building is less important than the manner in which it is built: The craftsman's joy and execution of his God-given talent by the work of his hands is what gives it its rare beauty and distinguishes it from just another building. *That we live* is not nearly as important as *how we live*.

The doctor I referred to previously, Henri Roca, has some interesting advice that will help keep us from suffering the same constipated way of living as the father of three. "We must learn to engage the world in an orgasmic manner. If we were to live each day as if we were in love with the day, we could generate untold amounts of energy, joy, and personal satisfaction. Witness the act of falling in love, or even falling into infatuation. Those in love have a glow about them. They are connected to the universal source of life and living. They are connected and in that connectedness are reunited with the universal source of limitless energy. Living each day with a sacred sexual connection keeps us linked to each other and to God."

Perhaps it's the misunderstanding of this basic concept of life that keeps people like our father of three in a constant state of anxiety and unhappiness. Instead of living in and enjoying the moment, they allow their shortsightedness to keep them from experiencing the real joys of life. In their rushing about, they focus on the events lying dimly in the distance while overlooking the riches that are clearly at hand. The message is simple: live in and enjoy the present — the experience is priceless.

Learn to Focus on the Light Hidden in the Darkness

It's hard to focus on the beauty of the bayou when you're up to your ass in alligators. We need to distance ourselves from the things nipping at our, ugh, "attention" before we can ever hope to discover the gifts that are hidden in our troubles. Nature provides us with such a vehicle in the passage of time. It is worth our while to be thankful for the healing we receive through the passage of time, because it helps take enough bite out of the sting so that we can see the truth in the shadows.

My friend Magnus is a professional photographer. I enjoy spending time with him for two reasons; first, he is a very talented and interesting person to converse with and second, if I whine enough, he lets me play with his expensive photography equipment.

During a visit to his shop, Magnus shared a story with me about a job he was engaged with at the time. A local manufacturer had commissioned him to photograph a new flight simulator, a computerized contraption used to train pilots how to fly. But for some reason, Magnus was having an inordinate amount of difficulty with the project.

"The lighting is all wrong," he confessed. "I've hit this thing with every strobe light I own, but look," he said, as he handed me a stack of pictures, each of which bore a striking resemblance to a huge scoop of vanilla Häagen-Dazs sitting atop a snow pile in a driving blizzard.

"Interesting," I said, handing the pictures back to him, "What is this supposed to be?" "Exactly," he responded, a shade of disgust in his voice. "So what's the problem?" I asked. "I wish I knew," he said, "I wish I knew...."

About a month later, I was back in Magnus's shop. "Put that down before you break it," I heard a familiar voice yell, "and come over here. I want to show you something."

I turned sheepishly around and saw Magnus standing there with a stack of photos in his hands. "Remember that flight simulator I told you about?" I nodded. "Well take a look at these," he said as he handed the pictures to me.

This set of pictures was much different than the first. Each one showed, in splendid detail, the intricacies of the subject. It was indeed something to behold, truly a thing of beauty.

So, what had been the problem? "Shadows — contrast," he replied. "There wasn't any in the first set of pictures." The problem, he explained, was that he was using too much light. "The subject in a photograph is like life itself," Magnus explained. "The beauty is revealed only when a little darkness falls onto it."

I don't know where Magnus learned his philosophy, but was he ever on the mark. We would never know the exuberance of success if it were not for its contrasting failures. We could not truly appreciate pleasure without first knowing pain. Like iron exposed to the weather, painful experiences rust our spirits into things of soulful beauty.

Think for a moment about everything ever invented. Didn't things that were once considered problems sire many of these inventions? Problems and crises fuel the creative fires, and the greater the amount of fuel, the more brilliant the flame. Crises can be the inspiration for many a life-changing move made by a servant leader.

When I first met my friend Evelyn Glennie, I knew there was something special about her. I watched her from the wings as she rehearsed with the symphony orchestra that was to accompany her in that evening's performance. There she was, standing at front-center stage explaining to the 105 members of the orchestra and its conductor the feeling she wanted to convey to the audience at the closing of her final number. Everyone on stage, as well as all within earshot, seemed to hang on every word she uttered — she is that charismatic. No, Evelyn is not a singer, she is a soloist — a solo percussionist.

Now, just in case you are not an aficionado of classical music, let me tell you percussionists do not normally take on the role of a soloist. In this respect, Evelyn is not only the best in her field; she has also earned the distinction of being the first in her field.

This talented, Scottish-born composer and performer is more than just another drummer girl. Evelyn has earned the distinction of being the first full-time solo percussionist in classical music history, and, as such, she has performed with the world's most-celebrated orchestras, chamber groups, and singers. At some of her concerts she has played as many as a dozen different instruments, some of the five hundred or so traditional instruments from Japan, India, Brazil, Korea, and Indonesia that comprise her personal collection.

Even her bare-footed performance style is unique. *New York Times* critic John Rockwell described her performance in a review of October 3, 1993, as follows: "She leaps about the stage like a pixie...with an engaging combination of athleticism and musicianship." Evelyn's unique style has created what the London *Independent* called "almost...a new type of musical theater."

Following her concert with the Philharmonic in 1996, the *New York Times* music critic James R. Oestreich wrote, "[her performance] may well stand as the most thrilling moment of the New York Philharmonic season," and referred to Evelyn Glennie as "quite simply a phenomenon as a performer."

Evelyn Glennie, along with her talented husband Greg, has

composed scores for film, theater, and television. Evelyn has recorded eight solo albums, published an autobiography, *Good Vibrations* (Thorndike Large Print, 1990), when she was just twenty-four, and has been the subject of at least three television documentaries. She has received many prestigious honors and awards. To fulfill her role as a servant leader, Evelyn shares her musical genius with up-and-coming percussionists the world over through her university-sponsored master classes. With the aid of her husband Greg and his prowess for high-tech, Evelyn launched the first "virtual percussion master class" on the Internet.

Evelyn has amassed quite a remarkable list of accomplishments for a woman in her early thirties. But what makes her musical accomplishments even more amazing is what radio legend Paul Harvey would call "the rest of the story." Evelyn Glennie is profoundly deaf and has been since an illness took her hearing at the young age of twelve.

What could Evelyn Glennie have accomplished had her hearing not been lost at an early age? If you were to ask, she would tell you, "not nearly as much!"

In her autobiography, Evelyn writes: "It didn't disappoint me to learn that no surgery or hearing aid currently available was going to restore me to good hearing. I had learned to cope with my silent world and felt that my own ways of listening to music gave me a sensitivity that I far preferred to the 'normal' way of hearing that I experienced as a tiny child. Because I had to concentrate with every fiber of my body and brain, I experienced music with a profundity that I felt was God-given and precious. I didn't want to lose that special gift."

I once asked Evelyn, if, sometime in the future, a medical breakthrough would make it possible for her to hear again, she would avail herself of it: "My deafness is something unique, I treasure it and don't want it to be taken away; no, I would prefer to stay as I am."

Due to her profound musical talents and her ability to carry on a virtually "normal" conversation, most people remain completely unaware of her hearing impairment. And if it were up to Evelyn, that is how it would stay. She prefers to be known as a woman who is single-handedly changing the face of classical music and not, as she puts it, "some plucky little deaf girl." I know Evelyn in a different light than most, as the embodiment of a true servant leader. She commits her gentleness and compassion to serve others' needs in ways only she can.

During a recent visit, I asked Evelyn why she chose music as a means of expressing her artistic gifts. Certainly, her choice resulted in a lot of personal pain, ridicule, and rejection in the early days. She answered in a way I had predicted, a way many might find illogical; a particular trait of servant leaders is to choose a path that makes the least sense of all, but it's one they know in their heart is the right one. In Evelyn's case, her destiny was to become a musician instead of a painter, sculptor, or, as one well-meaning relative once suggested, an accountant.

Evelyn's answer to my question was simple: "As a tiny child, music brought me such joy and peace. Anytime I was feeling bad, music was what took away the hurt. I wanted to give that same gift to people, no matter how hard it was going to be for me."

Evelyn's legacy can be found in her decision to look at her deafness as "a special gift." So many of us could benefit from that point of view.

I think you can see how Evelyn's focus on serving the needs of others worked to obliterate the possible devastating effects that her sudden hearing loss could have had in her life.

Is there a problem in your life that could be a blessing in

disguise? Are you, like my photographer friend, using too much of your energy to illuminate what you perceive as your good qualities and discounting the magic hidden in the shadows of your life? Is there a painful experience in your life that you can leverage, as my businesswoman friend did with her early childhood humiliation, to make you superior in some other aspect of your life? What "special gifts" have you been given that you can use to achieve greatness, like Evelyn Glennie?

Bad things are going to happen to good people, that is an indisputable fact of life. And when crisis besets us, we can either allow it to hold us down or we can use it to lift us up.

Going Further into Hell to Find Your Peace

If we live long enough, we will all experience our share of the good, the bad, and the ugly. The ugly I speak of are those events, circumstances, decisions, actions, and character traits that we feel are so awkward and uncomfortable that we keep them under wraps, away from the peering eyes of all who know us. We spend a great deal of energy concealing the ugly little bits of information about ourselves we feel are not fit for public view — too much energy, in fact.

I've always thought of it like trying to hold a beach ball underwater. Depending on the size of the ball, it could take all the strength we can muster just to keep the ball under control and from shooting out of the water — into the plain view of others.

As is often the case, what we feel is so ugly about us is not that bad after all. Sometimes our greatest strengths emerge as a result of our most painful and ugliest experiences. But, they will only come to the surface if and when we let everything else about us surface. When we let go of the ball, we regain the power it took to hold it down. Free from the encumbrances that have limited our personal growth — sometimes for decades — we can apply our newly found surplus of strength to serving the needs of others. We're simply transferring energy from evil — which would have us feel bad about ourselves in an attempt to keep us from attaining our rightful gifts in life — to something good.

I know a little something about how much effort it takes to keep that beach ball of life out of view from the world. Until very recently, I carried with me a part of my past that I held very close to my chest, for fear it would be exposed to the world and result in great personal humiliation. Although the period of time was brief, the events associated with it would have a major impact on shaping my character and defining the role that I live today. I look back at this period of time as both a blessing and a curse. The knowledge I would gain and the price I would pay for the education would serve to be both my most haunting apparition and most powerful ally.

The events I am speaking of took place when I was not quite twenty years old. At the time, I was living out of the backseat of a ten-year-old forest green Ford Thunderbird, with three hubcaps, bald tires, and bad brakes — that is, until my car was stolen, along with all of my possessions, from the parking lot of the place where I worked.

The Day the Bottom Fell Out

An icy winter rain fell, soaking through the thin, well-worn denim jacket that sparingly covered my bony frame. I stood staring emotionless at the empty parking space, where only eight hours earlier, at the beginning of the night shift, I had left my car. Exhausted, I collapsed onto the curb. The frigid gutter water soaked through my shoes, stinging my skin as I sat too weak to care, eyes fixed in a blank stare, senses tangled in paralyzing knots of despair. My world was ripping apart at the seams.

The early morning edition's headline peaked through the sun-yellowed window of the sidewalk vending machine: "Recession: No End in Sight." Just below the lead story another headline warned: "Only Two Holiday Shopping Days Left." Neither news story mattered very much to me — not much at all seemed to matter at that moment. I was drowning in a sea of hopelessness and self-pity.

My health was not good; I was suffering from the transient effects of ulcerative colitis (a debilitating intestinal disorder that causes severe abdominal spasms, painful cramping, and uncontrollable bouts of diarrhea) and blinding migraine headaches. The doctors at the hospital where I worked as an orderly said my maladies were most likely due to stress. "You're only a teenager, son," one doctor at the employee health clinic once commented. "What kind of stress could you have in your life?"

I closed my eyes and clenched my jaw, struggling to hold back the tears. This was the final blow. I had hit the very bottom of my life. And then the bottom fell out.

Negative thoughts and emotions flooded my mind. What's the use, I thought. I'll never make it; I don't have the strength anymore. Maybe I just don't deserve anything good in my miserable life. Engrossed in self-pity, I sat unfolding the story of my life, letting it play like a motion picture on the private silver screen behind my eyes.

I recalled the joy of Christmases past — the air filled with anticipation of holiday festivities, the sights, the sounds, the smells, the simple, comforting warmth of home.

Dad died when I was just a boy. The meager insurance policy he carried on his life was just about enough to cover his funeral expenses. Mom, a registered nurse, was left with three kids, a new mortgage, a stack of unpaid bills, and a broken heart.

After Dad died, I floundered aimlessly through life, getting into trouble wherever I could. There seemed little I could do right — forever swerving along the straight and narrow. When I was fourteen, Mom used her connections to get me an after-school job working as an orderly at the local hospital. That's where I met the first of many servant leaders who would influence my life.

Dr. James Gallo was a giant of a man who, however, stood a mere five foot four inches tall. A world-renowned cancer surgeon, Dr. Gallo, then retired, kept active by working part-time in the emergency room to which I had been assigned. By all accounts, Dr. Gallo was a success. He and his wife shared a fifty-two-room mansion in the exclusive community of Tuxedo Park, New York. One of the first Italian-Americans to graduate from the prestigious Columbia University College of Physicians and Surgeons, he went on to establish one of the first tumor clinics in the United States. He enjoyed warm admiration and respect from both his colleagues and the patients he served. He found life, love, hope, and happiness in his work, and his work brought these same gifts to thousands of other people.

During the lulls of the chaotic emergency department, he and I engaged in long conversations. He told me many stories of his life, of how he was born into poverty, grew up in an oppressive ghetto in New York City, battled the discrimination and hatred directed toward Italian immigrants, and struggled his way through college during the Great Depression that gripped the world in the 1930s.

Through his stories and actions, Dr. Gallo revealed to me the gifts awaiting those who dare to use their lives in service to others. He taught me the most valuable lesson of my life: All things are possible to those who discover their own unique way of serving others.

When I left high school, I began working three jobs, one full-time and two part-time, while carrying a full load of credits at college. I kept a small apartment not far from work, and I had saved enough money to buy a secondhand sofa bed and an inexpensive stereo. I was proudly moving ahead on my own steam, things were going my way. And then, bit by bit, the pieces to my happy puzzle started coming unglued.

The recession of the seventies was raging. Ph.D.'s were driving cabs and waiting tables. Companies everywhere were firing thousands of workers just to survive, and I became one of the statistics.

Two weeks after I lost my only full-time job, my apartment was burglarized, and there went my new furnishings. I was forced to go back to sleeping on the floor. And for my musical entertainment, I began once again listening to the muffled wails of Johnny Cash emanating from the paper-thin wall between my apartment and that of the building's superintendent, an affable, lanky man in his mid-forties named Jim.

Two months had passed since I lost my high-paying factory job, and my money was running out fast. I went back to the only work I knew how to do, that of a hospital orderly. But the only position I could find was at night, and it was part-time.

College tuition, books, and the few bad habits I had acquired — like eating — were rapidly depleting what little cash reserve I had managed to accumulate. My part-time, minimum wage paychecks seemed always to run out before the rent was due.

One too many latex rent checks and my landlord convinced me that it would be in the best interest of all for me to "make other living arrangements." That's when I moved into my car. And it was there that I "lived" until my car was stolen, along with all my personal possessions, on that cold and bleak

December night. In one sweep of the reaper's blade, I was homeless, carless, and stuffless — three strikes and you're out!

Running home to Mom was not an option. No one, not friends nor family, knew of my plight, and that is how I wanted it to stay. My pride was much larger than my intellect at the time. I always led everyone to believe that I was doing fine. Besides, I figured, Mom had enough to worry about without having to worry about me, too.

I had reached the lowest level in my young life. There I sat, in the gutter, cold, hungry, retching, and writhing in pain from a sickening migraine headache, and now homeless with nothing left but the clothes on my back.

Living on the streets wasn't easy, especially for a naïve, semi-sheltered boy from the suburbs. To survive, I needed to gain a whole new education and develop a whole new set of skills — like finding free, safe places to sleep and shower, how to eat for free or at little cost, and how to keep from getting attacked, robbed, or killed. The hardest thing I had to do was lie. I had to keep up an image of status quo, no matter what the cost. Not too many employers are happy to have an "itinerant bum" on their payroll. As for my friends, I slowly drifted apart from the few friends I had at the time. I felt it was too dangerous to hang around with the same people all of the time, for fear someone might ask to drop by my apartment or something like that. The super of my old building was nice enough to allow me to keep my mail coming to the building, where he would hold it for me until I picked it up.

I learned a lot about life during that time. I found, as all of us have at one time or another in our lives, that I was far more resilient than I had ever thought and capable of doing more than I ever gave myself credit for. I also developed a kind of sixth sense about people: who you could trust and who you couldn't. You had to determine — often in a split second — if the stranger walking toward you on that dark street was there to help you or harm you.

It was an education all right, one that I never would have chosen for myself, and certainly one I never wanted to share with anyone. That's why I worked so hard to keep this part of my life a secret from everyone, including those closest to me.

It's a hard thing to tell your wife, that the guy she married used to eat from garbage cans and often went days without bathing. Plus, I really didn't want to think of the impact my checkered history might have on the well-cultivated relationships I had developed with business associates and clients — most of whom possessed Ivy League degrees and social pedigrees to match. My past was simply a painful secret I had to keep.

Unfortunately, the weight of keeping secrets of this magnitude tends to get heavier as we grow older. The problem with keeping a piece of us under wraps and tightly guarded is we can never have the opportunity to bring it out in the open, where we can deal with it effectively and objectively. Hiding the problem, especially from ourself, negates our ability to critically analyze it and the effects it is having on our life and relationships. The survival mind-set that served me so well on the streets was keeping me from ever finding my potential as a servant leader.

When you are operating in a survival mode, your focus is on accumulating whatever you can at whatever cost. I treated people in a way that now sickens me, capitalizing on every opportunity that presented itself to me, no matter how it affected those around me. I did business in ways that benefited only me. If other people were diminished as a result, I figured it was simply their problem. I looked at people for what they could do for me, not what I could do for them. As a consequence, I was living a life that was the complete antithesis of servant leadership — and I was miserable for doing so.

This self-centered, survivalist approach to life was, I'm sure, at the root of many of the physical, emotional, and spiritual maladies I suffered over the years. Not until the darker years of my life were exposed to public view was I able to see how selfish and ruthless my behavior had become. In the process of concealing part of who I was and where I had traveled, I had become my own worst obstacle in the pursuit of my role as a servant leader.

The added burdens I had placed on myself by keeping a part of me hidden had no doubt adversely affected my work, my relationships, my self-image, my sense of inner peace, and a whole lot more. Yet, time after time, I desperately fought the need to give it up and let the ball go.

It was through the development of this servant leadership material that I was finally able to release the yoke that was holding me down all those years. Once I did, my whole world began changing in ways I had never thought possible.

I share this painful part of my past with you for only one reason, because each of us has a part of ourself that we feel is too ugly to be shown to the world. Keeping that something hidden from view is holding us back. Although your ugly parts might not be as homely as the part of me I shared with you, the results are the same. You are spending precious energy that you could be using for doing good rather than doing harm to yourself and those around you.

So, just let go of the ball; or, as my friend Juanell Teague from Dallas, Texas, likes to put it, "honey, ya just gotta tell the truth — quicker faster." I promise you your whole world will change for the better when you do.

CHAPTER 9

Allowing the Soul to Guide the Way

Of all the dimensions of humanity, it can be argued that the spiritual side is the most powerful. It is also the most mystifying. And, although we know very little of how our spiritual side works, we do know something of the richness it brings to living.

We have all experienced, on a spiritual level, our share of highs and lows, gains and losses. We have all tasted the sweetness of victory, shared in the treasures of accomplishment, and felt the pain and hopelessness of defeat. We have all experienced the fulfilling oneness that occurs between ourselves and others when we instantly "connect" with one another, and we have all suffered the deep, dull ache of loneliness. We have all experienced, if only for a fleeting moment, each of the spiritual wonders life has to offer, like the smell of the air just after a thunderstorm or the sweet tranquility of a cool late-summer's night. Each of us has, at least once in our lives, experienced an almost orgasmic spiritual synchronicity between us and the universe, as if the universe is magically working for us — like when every traffic light on your way home suddenly goes green as you approach.

We have all, too, from time to time, felt an uneasiness about us, an internal pulling away from where we are headed and toward a new and often frightening direction. This feeling of unrest, like the feelings of joy and peace we experience, seems to emanate simultaneously from all points around us and from deep within our core.

All of these feelings — tranquility and unrest, joy and pain, synchronicity and discord — originate from the same source: our soul. The human soul is both the nexus that connects humanity to its spiritual side and an internal guidance system designed to keep us on the road of our life's purpose.

What is your life's purpose? Although the methods we employ are as varied as the number of people on earth, the universal purpose of humanity, from the standpoint of the desires of the universe, is to use life to serve each other. As evidence, I offer my own observations. To put it as plainly as I can: when I focus my attention on serving others, my life is golden. When I allow the selfish, "survival" part of my natural self to dictate my life, my life turns to a shambles.

When we engage ourselves in the act of serving others, we experience a level of personal fulfillment unattainable by any other method. The feeling we get from serving others can be expressed in the phrase "our life's meaning," in that serving the needs of others brings meaning to our own lives.

It is this feeling of meaning in our lives that puts the "life" in our living. It's what makes us feel fulfilled, joyful, satisfied — worthwhile. Meaning brings purpose to our lives and to our work. Without it, we feel empty inside.

Recall the story of Dr. Frankl, the former prisoner of a Nazi death camp and pioneer in the field of logotherapy. During his tenure in hell, Frankl had the opportunity to observe, firsthand, the behavior of human beings forced to endure inhumane conditions.

Some of these wretched souls survived — most did not — but why? That was the question that would drive Frankl to discover how vitally important this thing dwelling deep inside the human spirit, this thing called meaning, is in the life of a human being. Frankl observed that survival had little to do with physical strength. In fact, quite the opposite seemed to be true. Survival, he found, was determined more by a person's ability to find meaning and purpose in life than any other factor.

Life in Our Meaning and Meaning in Our Life

Frankl's work shows that *meaning* is the most important thing in a person's life. When we lose meaning in our lives, we lose our *joie de vivre*, our very enthusiasm for living. If this absence of purpose and meaning, or even the prospect of it, is allowed to take hold, we might, as the prisoners in the death camps did, give up on life itself.

It's easy to lose sight of the sense of meaning in our lives if all we concentrate on is our own struggle and existence. Frankl stated that he owed his own survival to finding meaning in his suffering and in his ability to extend his focus beyond himself to the needs of those around him. Frankl's rock-solid commitment to serving the needs of others enabled him to put aside his personal suffering and take up the study of mankind, so that he might discover the hidden benefits behind the otherwise senseless atrocities that surrounded him. The meaning he derived from his work served Frankl like a life raft in a sea of madness, despair, and death.

The sense of meaning we get from our work, if we are truly using it to serve the needs of others, can be the very thing that breathes new life into an otherwise workaday job. If we lose sight of the real reason we do what we do, meaning can insidiously slip from our lives before we even know it. This happens when we yield to our natural tendency to focus our attention on ourselves and on the never-ending stream of problems that seem to come our way.

Not long ago, I was in the offices of Wanda Pearlmann, a client of mine. Wanda is a home-health-care administrator, and a darn good one at that. We were talking about this very subject, and she related the following story.

Wanda confessed to me that she had been feeling pretty low a while back. She remembered a particular day as being the bottom of her low point. It was the middle of the morning and she had not even looked at the stack of new messages looming on her desk. The telephone had been ringing all morning with nothing but problems on the other end. All of us can relate to what she must have been feeling.

The job that she once loved had become an endless maze of meaningless tasks. Work was piling up and morale was low. The daily tasks of having to do more and more with less and less were finally taking their toll. A beam of noonday sunlight making its way through her office window found this normally vibrant, highly committed, competent manager sitting in her chair, her head in her hands, weeping uncontrollably. "What the hell am I killing myself for?" Wanda thought.

The buzz of the intercom interrupted her little pity party. An unexpected visitor was waiting to see her. Wanda opened her office door and saw, sitting in the waiting room, a man in his mid-twenties with an infant boy. She introduced herself and the man, without warning, jumped from his chair and embraced her.

The young man, with tears in his eyes, explained: "I just wanted to say thank you for what you did for my family. He told her his name, and it all came rushing back to her. They had never met, he was just another voice on the other end of the phone. His wife of two years was dying of a brain tumor. She was just twenty-three years old. The young man and his new bride had just given birth to a son when her cancer was diagnosed and pronounced terminal.

Wanda recalled that her agency had to fight with the young man's insurance company to get even the most basic home health care approved. It was just another case, not much different from the thousands before.

The young man told her that, because of her efforts, he and his wife were able to share her few last months on this earth in peace and love. His young wife was able to leave this world surrounded by the ones she loved in the comfort of her own home, and not alone in some sterile hospital room.

Wanda began to weep as the man told his story. All at once, she saw standing in front of her the *meaning* in her work and the purpose in her life. A wave of peace flowed over her and suddenly she felt healed inside.

"For the rest of the day I was walking on air," Wanda said. "I passed on the young man's message of thanks to my nursing staff and as I did, I could see the gleam of meaning return to their eyes, too. I think we all need to feel our lives have meaning — that our struggle and efforts matter to someone other than ourselves."

You're Gonna Do Something Special Today

Finding an intense degree of meaning in our work is not limited to those in the health-care and helping professions. I know a toll collector who makes it a point to greet everyone who passes through his busy booth with a warm smile and a sincere word of encouragement, like the ones he had for me just this morning: "Something tells me you're gonna do something special today."

When I stopped to ask him about his approach to what most of us would call a mundane job, he answered: "My grand-daddy always told me, 'Sonny, if you treat every person you meet as if they were hurting deep inside, you'd be right most all of the time.' I never forgot that. So, that's why I do what I do. Ya just never know what's goin' on in a person's life. The way I see it, a few well-timed, unexpected words of encourage-ment can go a long way in making someone feel good inside — and I know it makes me feel great inside when I hand 'em out!"

Sonny's quite a guy, and the epitome of a servant leader. A friend of his once told me Sonny often helps young, inner-city kids learn to read on his off time, and can even be found visit-ing strangers at a retirement home not far from where he lives. But I'm sure even chronic optimists like Sonny have their down times, just as we mortals do.

Whether or not we are willing to admit it, each of us, from time to time, loses our sense of meaning. We have allowed our-selves to be driven off course by the forces of nature and our changing world. The winds of change and the blinding fog of life's nagging problems can trigger our survival instincts to kick in, pushing us off course in our desire to serve others and toward serving ourselves. If we continue moving in the direction nature and happenstance would have us move, like a rudderless ship lost in the dark along a rocky coast, we are surely headed for disaster.

Looking in All the Wrong Places

The problem most of us have when we find the meaning being leeched out of our life is that we look to recover it in all the wrong ways and in all the wrong places. We search for the meaning to our life in the things familiar to us — in our positions of authority, social standing, roles, in our goals and achievements, and in those material possessions that we collect and so dearly treasure. When we do this, we are setting the stage for an even greater acceleration toward meaninglessness, disappointment, and despair.

This is because all of the things we unsuspectingly lash our life's meaning to will soon change and often disappear. Change is inevitable. The universe is changing all the time and in every way. And, although we sometimes wish we could stop it, there's nothing we can do.

Mothers who place their whole stock of self-meaning in raising their kids are in trouble the minute those kids suddenly don't need them any longer. The same can be said about men and women who draw all their meaning from their careers and relationships.

Then there are those who, out of desperation, misguidedly fall victim to the endless parade of success gurus, who, out of their own misguided ignorance, teach people to link their entire life's meaning to their achievements. But achievements, once attained, are ineffective as vehicles for purpose and meaning. *Meaning* and *purpose* can only be found in the struggle, the *striving*, to reach one's goals.

I once heard a story about an army general, a brilliant strategist who lived his entire life needing to prove his intellectual and military superiority. The flawless execution of his brilliantly contrived sorties enabled his army to win the war and made him a hero among his peers.

He won the war, but, with his lifelong mission complete, he lost his purpose for living. As the story goes, he was last seen climbing to the top of the highest cliff, where he threw himself to his death.

We must never link our entire sense of meaning to static things and ideals. We must attach the purpose of our life to a vision that is malleable and adaptable to the changing universe around us.

Wouldn't it be wonderful if we had a life's purpose so powerful it would never let us sink into the black abyss of meaninglessness again? And, wouldn't it be great if we had some sort of internal warning device that could tell us when we had drifted off the course and could guide us back again? I propose we do in fact have both of these things.

If Life Is a Puzzle, We Are the Pieces

Everything in the universe has a purpose, a reason for being (excepting possibly tonsils and politicians). Consider for a moment the analogy of life as a jigsaw puzzle and you and me as the pieces. No two pieces in a jigsaw puzzle are exactly the same shape, size, or color. Each piece is unique. The same can be said about us. No two of us ever born have ever been exactly the same. We are all far more complex than we appear to be.

What makes us unique is hidden deep below our exterior. The things about us that will make the most difference in our lives are unseen, most times even by us.

A single piece of the jigsaw puzzle is not meant to exist on its own. Each piece of the puzzle has its unique place in the whole. Without each piece taking its rightful position, the entire puzzle is left incomplete. Only when all the individual pieces are fitted together do they create a coherent whole with substance and meaning. The same holds true for us. Together we interlock our differences — your strengths perfectly filling my weaknesses — melding together to form something so much more solid, powerful, and functional than any single part of the whole.

Next, we need to consider the matter of *perspective*. The closer we stand to our jigsaw puzzle, the less able we are to see the whole. Move closer still, and nothing at all makes sense. Only from a distance does the full picture come into view. This is also true about life and our role in it.

From our perspective, it is impossible to view the larger design of the universe that surrounds us. We are not privy to the grand order of things, how seemingly unconnected events and people are in fact working in concert to carry out a specific end. We are blinded to what lies in the distance by the myopic view we hold of our own existence. This is why we often stumble around and lose our way, to end up interminably frustrated.

Let Your Soul Be Your Guide

Because of our nearsighted view of life and our role in it, the only way for us to fulfill the purpose for which we have been designed — which is to serve each other in a unique way with our predestined talents, strengths, experiences, and resources — is to receive our guidance from a source with a perspective that is much higher than our own.

How do we tap into this all-seeing, all-knowing force that governs the universe? For assistance, we can turn to the soul. The soul can see the answers to our life's purpose because it is looking at our life from a different perspective.

When we stray off course, our actions may go unnoticed by our conscious mind, but they never go unnoticed by the soul. The unexplainable uneasiness we often feel is simply the calling of our own soul, beckoning to us, as a lighthouse beacon warns us away from the rocky shore. Like that rudderless ship on a moonless night, we have lost our way, and our soul is calling out to us to guide us back to safety.

If we are ever to find our rightful place in this great puzzle called life, we must learn to connect with, hear, and accept the guidance of our soul. Sadly, those who know no better will simply ignore the calling, thinking that they are in control of their life. Like we once did, they will continue to cling to their self-centered convictions, pressing blindly onward with outdated charts through the darkness of change.

It seems not to matter to most people; they have lost the guiding beacon. Why doesn't it matter? I guess it's because we are just too proud of the course we have chosen for ourselves. So we stay our course and block out the internal warnings, pretending they are not there, and all the while the clang of the warning bell grows louder.

When we fall victim to these tendencies, we end up on the rocks, just like those who ignored the warnings before us. We curse the jagged rocks and blame God or fate for a consequence of our own design. It's not as if the real reasons behind our dilemmas, or the steps we should have taken to avoid them, completely elude us. We often know what we *should have done* all along; we just choose not to do it, and this is when our soul calls out to us the loudest.

What is it about the human condition that keeps us from doing what we know in our hearts and souls we should do? It's simple: to do what we know we should do would require *change*. Change is the hardest thing for a person to do. Why? Perhaps because our sense of meaning is rooted in inappropriate beliefs and the choices we have made.

To "change" would be, in our minds, like giving up part of who we are, to forfeit our entire sense of meaning. If we stay rooted in our present decisions and choices, refusing to acknowledge the changing universe around us, we will surely lose this precious meaning anyhow. So, is our quest for servant leadership a hopeless catch-22? No. But it does require us to accept guidance from a level higher than that within ourselves.

Two abilities that separate humans from other animals are the gift of reason and the ability to think outside ourselves. Inherent in these gifts is the need to use them. If we attempt to fool ourselves into believing we can guide ourselves through the maze of life without the aid of an "outside" source, we condemn ourselves to a future of running headstrong into the pitfalls and obstacles that have plagued us in the past. At the very least, we will surely miss the true rewards that await all who dare to walk the path of service. We must learn to turn outside ourselves and go beyond our limited realm of control and experience to discover an easier path to our life's rewards. But where do we turn?

If you are traveling with a guide, you don't need a map. If we learn to accept guidance from a higher, spiritual level, we can put aside the earthly notion that we must know every twist and turn along the way before we even begin the journey. By tapping into the spiritual side of our humanity, we open a connection with all others, living and past, and with the powers that control the machinery of the universe. When we learn how to use our soul to link us to the source of infinite intelligence, we no longer need any other form of guidance.

Connecting with the source of infinite intelligence is more about *being* than it is about *doing*. The less we try to control the experience, and the more we simply allow it to happen, the more effective and regular the connection becomes. This state of being and connection with the universal source of wisdom can only be accomplished when we choose to put aside our need for self-control and trust a higher power exclusively to guide our life. If we have any hope of receiving guidance from this omnipotent source of wisdom, we need to learn to open and maintain a clear channel of communication. In the following pages I will share with you a few of the favorite methods that have helped me and many of the servant leaders I have worked with to open and maintain that channel of communication.

The decision to accept and employ these or other methods is yours alone. All I can do is suggest that you employ some method that opens you to the wisdom and guidance that can change your life. Unless and until you do so, nothing will be any different.

It has been said that we are not physical beings with a spiritual side, but rather spiritual beings that have taken physical form. For each new gray hair that appears on my beard, I come one tick closer to this way of thinking.

We've already talked about how our soul is the guide to the spiritual side of our humanity. We've even discussed how the soul seeks us out and tries to guide us toward what is best for us. What we haven't touched on, however, is how we might learn to actively call upon the soul for guidance. But before we can go off in search of our soul and call upon it for help, we first need to learn a little bit about where it dwells and how we might speak to it in a language it might better understand.

Tearing Down the Wall Technology Built

For some reason, those of us who inhabit the more industrially developed nations of the world seem to believe that doing more will somehow yield us more. When we mistakenly enter into this thought pattern, we come dangerously close to mistaking activity for accomplishment. Despite what most of us have been unconsciously conditioned to believe, the two are not necessarily connected.

As I drove to the office this morning, a young woman reminded me of our propensity to cram every waking moment of our existence with projects and tasks in hopes that we might gain more control over our lives. The young woman was driving a car in the lane next to me. As we headed down the expressway, I couldn't help notice her: It was the first time I have ever seen anyone eat breakfast, talk on the phone, apply eye makeup, and sort through papers while driving a car at sixty-five miles per hour.

This woman wasn't alone in her pursuit of multitasking nirvana, either. The fellow driving just behind her was reading a newspaper, drinking coffee, and yelling at three arguing kids seated in the backseat. This perpetual multitasking is not a problem we succumb to only while driving. Just this morning, as I sat in Central Park enjoying the shade of a 200-year-old oak tree, I happened to catch sight of a jogger talking on his cell phone and fiddling with his Palm Pilot while he ran. Similar observations by friends in Europe and Asia suggest this is not just an American ill; it seems to be part of a worldwide phenomenon.

We're all too busy for our own good. Most of us live as if we will be judged at our final reckoning according to the number of crossed-off items on our cosmic to-do list. I'm not sure what it is that causes otherwise rational people to think that, by working harder, faster, and longer, they'll get everything done, when they know by experience the exact opposite is true.

Often the harder, faster, or longer we work at a task the less effective we become, and in most cases getting "everything done" is a human impossibility. We're just not built to move at the pace most of us tend to push ourselves to.

The technology we once thought would make our lives simpler is actually producing the obverse effect. Cell phones, PDAs (Personal Digital Assistants) with satellite capabilities, voice mail, E-mail, and the like, bring the world within our reach. Unfortunately, they also bring us within the reach of the world.

Our tender senses are assaulted every moment by billions of new and changing sights, sounds, smells, and other sensations. More information is hurled at our minds today than at any time in history, and we are reacting negatively to the overload. The human attention span is shrinking in response to the ever-increasing number of demands being placed on it, and our nerves are raw from wear. To maintain our sanity and preserve a small scrap of solitude, we learn to block most of the sensations that we deem nonessential. In consequence, all that is sensuous and spiritual ricochets off the impenetrable wall we have erected.

Such is another of life's follies: In a vain attempt to quiet our tired minds and draw closer to the sound of our souls, we strain out the very things that will bring us peace, joy, and the spiritual connection we seek. The absurdity is this: The more we fail in attaining peace through filtration, the harder we try. Until one day we have blocked so much from our lives, we find that we're not really living at all; we're merely alive.

In order to draw closer to our soul, we need less in our lives, not more. Instead of hurrying to fill the voids in our schedule with more activity, we need to take time to experience the sensual and spiritual side of life: We need to nourish the relationship with our soul and allow it to grow.

Sensuality is akin to the soul. We need to bring sensuality back into our everyday lives. When was the last time you lay in fresh-cut grass and felt the warmth of the sunshine on your face and the softness of the breeze on your skin? Can you remember the last time you spent the entire day in bed with your lover, or ate spaghetti with your hands?

We seem to be able to make time for everything else, but we need to make time for the sensual things in life, the things that really make life worth living. We need to make time for doing

nothing at all, so we can once again experience the joy of serenity. We need to slow down a bit, so we can become in synch with
nature. We need to feed our souls with sensuality, quiet, and
reflection so we can better communicate with God.

Meeting the Universe on Common Ground

Because God dwells deep within us, we need to allow ourselves the time to experience one another on a much deeper
level, to see the similarities rather than the differences, and to
get past the small talk and share with each other the deep
human experiences we all have every day.

To help us get to know each other better, we need to share
things like the gift of humor with each other. We also need to
take time to share an honest compliment or a simple hug with
everyone we meet. I believe these are the mechanisms by which
God's comfort can pass through our soul to the soul of another.

We need to tear down the walls that we have built between
our souls and the souls of others. Only then will we begin to see
a glimmer of evidence of the God that lives within all of us.

Walking in Rhythm

We are running ourselves ragged searching for the answers
to the matters of life. The folly is, the answers are right in front
of us all the while; but we will never find them until we stop
looking for them and simply allow them to find us. To accomplish this, we need to put on the brakes and slow down; we need
to get closer to the natural rhythm of life.

There is a certain rhythm to everything in the universe,
including human life. I'm not getting metaphysical with you;
I'm simply stating scientific fact. All living creatures live to a
certain natural rhythm. When we push ourselves to live at a
pace faster than what nature intended, we create discord.

Unmet needs have a habit of revealing themselves to us in often unexpected ways. The need for a slower life rhythm is no exception. We've all heard someone speak in reverence of the good old days, when, in theory at least, times were slower paced and life was simpler.

Products and services with a nostalgic appeal are growing in popularity at exponential rates. We're witnessing the return of the "milkman" and home-delivered groceries, many with a high-tech approach, such as a Web-based delivery service that promises to fetch a copy of your favorite video, a six-pack, and a pizza and deliver them to your door within an hour of your E-mail request. And, in this age of E-mail and PDAs, the fountain pen is making a huge comeback.

The gravitational pull on our souls to return to a more comfortable pace did not go unnoticed by Dante Del Vecchio, president of Visconti Pens of Florence, Italy. I asked Dante for his personal take on the consumer movement to recapture the past. "The world is moving too fast for most of us. Things that used to take weeks, even years, to develop now happen in just seconds. Nature's tendency is to right itself. For many people, the simple act of writing with an instrument as old as the fountain pen gives them a sense of slowing down a bit."

Destined for a life of public service, Dante gave up his political aspirations to form Visconti Pens in 1988. The story behind Dante's unique call to service is as interesting as the man himself. To fund his political science education at the university, Dante sold the secondhand automobile his parents gave him as a graduation present, then used the proceeds as a down payment on a stationery shop in Florence.

"Stationery held no magic for me. The shop was for sale, I

had the means of making the down payment, people need stationery — it was just that simple."

It was during his tenure as a shopkeeper that this part-inventor, part-artisan, part-businessman, part-politician first noticed a consumer demand for simplicity. Being young and innovative, Dante stocked the shop with all the latest electronic gadgets. The items sold moderately well, but Dante began to notice a trend beginning to emerge in his customer base. "A growing number of my customers were asking me for fountain pens — the expensive kind."

The closer Dante looked at this odd request coming from his customers, the more he could relate to an unmet need they all seemed to have: the need to slow the pace of life. Dante knew very little about fountain pens, except what he remembered from his school days. Teachers had made him write with a fountain pen in order to improve his penmanship. In those memories, he saw his destiny.

Dante sold his stationery shop, put his political science degree on the shelf, and began making pens. Today Visconti Pens is one of the most respected producers of fine writing instruments in the world.

Dante Del Vecchio is not the only astute businessperson I have ever met who has, in an odd sort of way, made a profitable business out of helping others regain a connection with their soul. Another example is John Conover, Sr. A third-generation farmer, John was forced to confront the possibility of losing his family farm fifteen years ago, when he realized he could no longer pay the bills.

"The cost of everything was going up, while at the same time the prices we could get for our crops were going down. We were in real jeopardy of losing this plot of ground that has been passed down through three generations. It ain't much to look at, but it means more to me than most things. I just could not let that happen, but I had no idea what I could do to stop it.

"Then one day a fellow stopped by and asked if he could buy one of the blue spruces that lined the outside of the corn-field. He said it would make the perfect Christmas tree for his family, and he would pay me thirty dollars for it. This price was the equivalent of what I might get for a wagon-load of corn. I hopped off my tractor and ran to the barn to get my ax."

That next spring, John and his son started planting Christmas trees instead of corn. Today, Conover Farms is one of the premier preselect tree growers in the greater New York area. John told me most of the customers he had fifteen years ago are still coming back, but now they bring their grandchildren along too. "I guess you could say we're really selling a tradition around here. People need to have a little bit of convention and stability in their lives — even if it's the simple act of picking out their own Christmas tree, cutting it down, and taking it home. People love it, too; you should see this place on opening day: Folks get here hours ahead of time just so they can get the pick of the crop, and the look on the kids' faces is pure heaven."

Moving too fast for our natural rhythm — and that includes being too busy — is not a healthy or satisfying way to live, nor is it conducive to a mental state that is needed to find the answer to anything.

A few months ago, I was standing in the airport check-in line, about to embark on an important business trip. At the time, I had to deal with a number of unexpected and troubling business and personal problems that seemed to come into my life all at once. Although the trip had been planned quite far in advance, it could not have come at a more inopportune time.

I usually get to the airport well ahead of time so I can spend some time relaxing and going over my thoughts for the day, but an overturned truck on the expressway and the resulting traffic backup put a crimp in my usual routine. I arrived at the airport feeling rushed and a bit anxious.

As I stood in line, I made a final check of my personal belongings: Wallet? Yup. Keys, briefcase, tickets? Check. Sunglasses? Sunglasses?? Sunglasses!

My prescription sunglasses were not in their case; they were neither in my briefcase nor in my suit pockets. *Great! This is just great!* I mumbled to myself in disgust. *Two weeks on the road without my glasses.* My eye doctor has told me repeatedly not to go into the bright sun without ultraviolet protection over my eyes — some eye condition with an ominous-sounding, seven-syllable name.

I must have left my glasses in the car, I thought. I glanced at my wristwatch. Hmm, nineteen minutes till boarding. It was going to be tight, but I had no choice other than to hop a shuttle bus back to the long-term parking lot, retrieve my sunglasses, catch another bus back to the terminal, and meet my plane before it left the ground.

The airport gods were with me that day. As soon as I exited the terminal door, I saw the outbound shuttle bus headed for the parking lot. Jumping aboard, I explained to the driver that I had left something in my car and had to retrieve it.

The bus driver — Mohammad was his name — came up with an ingenious plan: He would drop me at my car and then return to his normal route, where he would begin picking up passengers. I would go to my car, retrieve my glasses, and jog about five hundred feet to the closest bus stop, where Mohammad would pick me up and return me to the terminal in plenty of time to make my flight. I had about two minutes and thirty seconds to accomplish my part of the plan. No problem — or so I thought.

I opened the door to my car and looked inside, expecting to find my sunglasses sitting on the seat where I had left them. They were not there. Maybe they fell on the floor. Nope, not there either. I glanced at my watch — only sixty seconds left. That's about the time real panic began setting in. Small beads of sweat formed on my brow; my heart began to pound like I was running a marathon, and it felt like I was breathing liquid instead of air. I was on the verge of having an anxiety attack.

So, what did I do? I did the only seemingly logical thing a person could do in situations like these; I began ranting and raving like a lunatic. "This is just wonderful! Here I am going to miss my *stinking* plane because I can't remember where I left my *stinking* glasses." (Although "stinking" was not the actual word I was using; the real word was much stronger.)

I scrambled all over the floor of the car for the third time — still nothing. Exasperated and exhausted from the tension, I flopped into the driver's seat. "Forget it," I said to myself, looking at the dirty patches on the knees of my new suit. "I'll just have to do without."

Just then, I caught site of my pitiful self in the rearview mirror. There were my sunglasses — I was wearing them.

Now I know nothing like this has ever happened to you, unless of course you count the time you went on a tirade, accusing everyone of moving your car keys, only to find them in your hand.

So, what's my point? The answers we so desperately seek are often "hidden" in plain view, but you will never find them when you are under mental pressure. The answers can only come in the calm, for that is where the soul lives.

Calmness is not only a balm for the troubled mind and tired body, but also a powerful gateway to universal intelligence.

Calmness is the glue that binds together our physical, mental, and spiritual beings in a state of universal harmony, and it is the only state in which we can effectively shut down our cluttered minds and achieve the heightened level of consciousness necessary to communicate with the soul.

We need to develop an abundant surplus of calmness to draw from in times when we need it most. To accomplish this, we need to take time each day to practice being calm.

Finding Your Wondering Place

I'm convinced the main reason we do not find time to practice calmness and reflection is because we do not have a specific place in which to do it. We do not have what my friend Paul Breier calls a "wondering place."

Even if we have spent all our lives desiring to practice meditation and reflection, and had all the time we wanted in which to practice it, it would still be unlikely that we would actually do it unless we had a specific place to go that is conducive to meditation and reflection.

We have special places for just about everything in our lives — libraries for learning, houses of worship for prayer — why then not a place — a "wondering place" — for meditation and reflection?

We need a place to go to get away from the rest of the world and reflect on our own life and our roles in it. Everyone ought to carve out a special nook, the corner of an attic, a hidden place in the garden, a rock in the park, even a spot in the garage or basement, in which to be alone with their thoughts, a place in which we can communicate with our souls.

If we are ever to do any significant meditation and reflection, we need to find our own wondering place.

Connecting with the Spirit

The simple act of taking time for yourself can do a lot to bring calmness into your spirit and a more natural rhythm back into your life. Prayer, meditation, contemplation — whatever you want to term it — you need to devote a portion of your day to communicating with your soul. The time you spend at this activity does not have to be huge — five minutes a day is good enough to begin with; the critical part is making this activity part of your everyday routine.

Beginning today, carve out at least five minutes a day to do nothing but get in touch with the rhythm of nature; for example, leave home five minutes earlier and stop by a park or other quiet place.

Once there, sit quietly. If you are in your car, turn off the engine and the radio. Begin to relax by taking in large, deep breaths through your nose and exhaling slowly through your mouth. Do this deep-breathing exercise about five or six times, then simply sit quietly and try to get a feel for the rhythm of the world around you.

Now, begin breathing slowly through your nose, and with each inhalation of fresh air, mentally say the word "relax." As you slowly exhale, repeat the word "deeper." Inhale — relax, exhale — deeper. Repeat this a few times, until you can feel the tension flowing out of your body with each exhalation. As you breathe, close your eyes and picture a warm, healing light enveloping your body. As you bask in this healing light, listen to the sounds of nature: the calls of the birds and the wind rustling through the trees. Notice the rhythm these sounds seem to have.

Allow your breathing and internal sense of timing to regulate to this slower, methodical pace. Just sit quietly, adjusting to the rhythm of the universe for as long as you are able. Over time, you will find you are able to be quiet for longer periods of time.

Although this is certainly the best scenario, if going to a park does not work for you, try locking yourself in the bathroom or staying in the shower five minutes longer than usual. Where and when you carry out this routine is of lesser importance than that you actually do it every day.

Faithfully do this exercise each day for thirty days, and you will notice some interesting changes begin to happen in your life. To start with, you'll notice a deeper connection with your spiritual side begin to emerge. You'll begin to find more moments of peace included in your daily routine. Your ability to deal healthily with stress will be enhanced, as will your capacity to find new and creative solutions to problems that crop up in your life. Over time, you will find that you are able to think more clearly than in the past — and you just may save those few minutes you've been spending every month looking for your keys.

Daily meditation or prayer is a valuable tool for reestablishing our natural life rhythm, developing our ability to attain calmness on demand, and is also the key to developing an ongoing relationship with God — which is the primary goal of our spiritual development.

Servant leaders need to learn to live, not as a raging river, tumbling over the jagged rocks of life, but as a peaceful stream, carrying in their current the life-enhancing gifts of humor and encouragement to all they touch.

CHAPTER 10

Show Me the Money

I've often heard people say: "There is more to life than just money." They're right — there are stocks and bonds, negotiable securities, precious metals, gemstones, collectable art, and real estate too!

I've had money and I haven't had money, so I can tell you with honest certainty, it's better to have money than not to have it. The fact is, nothing can replace money for what money can do, but money alone is not the panacea everyone who lacks it tends to think it is.

Money is also not the ultimate problem solver many people think it is. The only problems that can be solved by having a bucketful of money are those needing a bucketful of money to solve.

People don't stop having problems because they are rich, as those who are not often think. Most times, wealthy people simply trade the problems associated with a lack of money for those associated with having a lot of money.

As many problems as having money can create, not having

it can be even more detrimental. Financial problems have caused more divorces than infidelity ever has. Money problems can lead us to disregard our health, cause us mental and emotional stress, and destroy our peace of mind.

Tragically, the main cause of most financial woes could have easily been avoided with just a basic education about the proper use and management of money. Money is something we need and use every day of our modern lives; yet, to so many of us, money is a mystery.

Angelo Facciponti, a financial consultant, says the following about money: "It amazes me how little people know about something they use every day of their lives. Most people haven't a clue how to manage their own finances. The subject is not taught in schools, and the knowledge is rarely passed from parent to child. Rather, it's left up to chance and trial and error. Perhaps that's why, with the stock markets of the world reaching daily record heights, personal bankruptcy is also at an all-time high. People are in too much debt for their own good."

Wealth building is also a concept that seems to be absent in the thoughts of the majority of people I meet. According to Facciponti, most people don't even begin thinking about their financial future until about the age of forty-eight. Another alarming commonality is the number of people I meet who spend the bulk of their paycheck before they even cash it — putting nothing away for emergencies or toward savings. If they even have a savings plan, the amount in it is usually limited to about a thousand dollars. One strong wind, and these people are ruined. Angelo reminds us that: "Earning money is only half of the story. Using the money you have earned to build wealth is the part most people miss. If they only knew how simple it was to change their condition . . ."

Angelo is right; it's easy to acquire money, especially in a free market–driven society. Working to earn money is, in fact, only part of the equation: Getting your money to work for you is the other part. And like Angelo suggests, it's not really that hard to do. But for most people, it will mean making a few changes. The first thing you may have to change is your attitude regarding money.

Developing an Attitude of Abundance

Having lived on both sides of the equation, I can tell you: the only difference between people who have money and people who don't is in the attitudes each group has toward money and the habits they form based on those attitudes.

The rich — and I'm not talking about the "newly rich" — look at money simply as a tool, for what it can accomplish for them. The poor look at money as a solution to their problems. Speaking from experience, the only people who think money will solve all of their problems are those who don't have any of it.

The rich tend to treat their money with cautious respect and a kind of reverence you would more likely expect to find in those who define themselves as struggling to make ends meet. If, for instance, you were to shop in a wealthy neighborhood, you would see a lot of coupon clipping, comparison shopping, and bargain hunting going on.

Watching what people buy with their money can also tell you a great deal about their attitude toward money, and proportionately about their potential for developing wealth. The differences are often as simple as those between *investing* and *spending*. The wealthy tend to *invest* their money in appreciating assets like real estate, stocks and bonds, precious metals, collectible art, and antiques. Those who are not wealthy *spend* their money on consumer goods such as fancy cars and clothes, elaborate vacations, and big-screen televisions equipped with every conceivable cable and satellite station.

Appreciating assets, such as those the wealthy tend to invest their money in, rise in value over time, making their owners even more money. Consumer goods, on the other hand, end up in the garbage dump — sending their owners back to the store for replacements.

The wealthy tend to never touch their principal net worth, the money they have earned and saved/invested. Instead, they tend to live in such a manner that they are able to live off of the interest their investments have made for them: They live well below their means. This means they are able to live debt free in most cases. Those who lack money spend every cent of their earnings — "that's what money's for, you have to spend it while you've got it," you'll often hear them say.

Of the many self-made millionaires I've known over the years, most don't buy new, expensive automobiles every year; rather, they tend to drive cars that are on average ten years old. They live in homes that are comfortable but not ostentatious. They tend to be married to the same mate. They have a deep sense of spirituality and belief in God; most regularly attend some type of religious service. Most, if not all, I've known regularly give a portion of their money to causes they feel very strongly about; they understand and practice a basic servant leader tenet: *You gotta give to get, and the more you give the more you'll get.* All tend to place importance on their wealth but do not have an obsession with it. Certainly, they don't talk about how much money they have to everyone they meet.

Conversely, people who do not have money tend to make that fact known to seemingly everyone. Money, or the lack of it, seems to be an obsession with them. No matter what happens in their lives, to them it's a result of a lack of money: "If I only had the money," they say. The sad fact is they most likely had the money but chose to squander it in an attempt to satisfy their insatiable craving for consumer goods.

Unlike most self-made millionaires, those who lack money tend to link their happiness to the possession of it and the material objects money can buy: "I'm only miserable because I'm broke; if I only had some money, then I'd be happy." Because of their obsession with the possession of money and the collection of material objects, the thought of regularly giving a portion of their money to fund a worthy cause is anathema to them; and so, the only return they can expect for their greed is more greed. In addition, this obsession, and the tendency to falsely link self-worth with material objects, serve only to drive them into debt and further into poverty. The wealthy tend not to risk their money on get-rich-quick schemes, highly speculative investments, or on gambling it away at casinos or the lotto. Those without money tend to do all of these things. So, there you have it — sort of a nutshell comparison of money handling habits and attitudes between the *haves* and the *have-nots*.

Since our attitudes toward money directly affect the habits we develop in the management of our money, it would be best for us to develop a healthy, servant leader–like attitude toward money. Just as we need to develop a healthy attitude with respect to maintaining a state of abundant wellness — changing our attitude from one of illness to wellness — we must also develop an attitude that is beneficial to our goal of financial abundance. We must cultivate an attitude that is *wealth conscious* rather than *poverty conscious*. We need to develop habits of *abundance* versus habits of *lack*.

Why all this talk about money? Because, in order to be effective as a servant leader, you will have to be as strong financially as you are physically, mentally, and spiritually.

Some time in the future, when you have developed an awareness for such things, you will be presented with what I've come to know as a "servant vision," which is typically a mission you alone are qualified to undertake and one you certainly never would have thought of yourself. There is no doubt in my mind that part of what you will need to fulfill that mission will be a strong and abundant financial base. Not having a strong financial base might eliminate the possibility of bringing that critical vision to fruition, thus causing you to miss perhaps your only opportunity to participate in a plan of universal proportions.

A woman I know had a vision to open a retreat house to serve as a sanctuary for parents who have recently lost a child. She knew firsthand the pain these parents were feeling and the strain that their loss would have on their marriage, having tragically lost her own infant son in an automobile accident.

This once determined woman would, however, let her vision go unfulfilled, because she was caught up in a lifestyle that had a voracious appetite for money and demanded to be fed continuously. She was living in a neighborhood that was well above her means, and as a result she had to "keep up appearances." So, as many people will do who are caught up in similar money traps, she leased a luxury car that she could not afford to buy and spent money that she could not afford to spend. In essence, she became a slave to her lifestyle. And there went the potential to make an impact in this world that she was uniquely qualified to make; and so went with it a potential benefit to an untold number of grieving parents.

We can choose to focus on serving either *our* needs or the needs of others; we can't serve both. When we choose to live in a way that sucks the life out of our dreams and visions of serving others, we end up serving no one, not even ourselves.

My friend is just another statistic in a long list of would-be servant leaders who have been misled by the seemingly endless hordes of so-called "success gurus," who tout the merits of living beyond your means as a method of forcing yourself to do better financially. The real truth is this: The only thing living beyond your means will get you is broke.

Greed Ain't Good

Living beyond our means, in addition to sapping our available resources, commandeering our free time, depleting our personal energy, and destroying our ability to fulfill our vision, can also cause us to become greedy. Greed, as we have heard from many a repentant Wall Street tycoon, is not as good as they had previously boasted it to be. Greed does not make good human sense, because it consumes our soul like a black hole — gobbling up all of our energy — and it doesn't make good business sense, either.

I have two friends, Tony and J. R. Both men have a lot in common: each is a successful businessman, has a vast network of influential and wealthy friends, and is constantly on the lookout for new and exciting business ventures. Both men are astute at reading people, and they have one more common bond: Each recently purchased a beautiful new home. This is where the similarities end.

What separates these two men are the builders of their homes, the experience with their respective builders, and the results. Tony's builder was an affable, talented young man just starting out in the building field. He had been building custom homes for about five years. J. R.'s builder was also talented and affable but had been in the business of building custom homes for about twenty years. He was also involved in a number of other business and real estate ventures.

From the very beginning, Tony felt at ease dealing with his

builder. Tony felt that, although his builder hoped to yield a generous profit from their business transaction, by and large the builder held both of their interests equally at hand. J. R., on the other hand, came away from his initial meeting with quite a different feeling toward his builder and their relationship together: "I felt as if I had to keep my hand over my wallet every time I was around the guy. I could tell he was capable of doing the job, but I also knew this guy bore watching." Both Tony and J. R. have proven themselves to be astute judges of people, and they have developed an uncanny ability to read into a business deal and come away on the good side of it.

When a structural problem occurred during the construction of Tony's home, his builder immediately exposed the problem to Tony and fixed it without a second thought. Given the nature of most defects, the builder could have easily covered up the problem or passed the additional cost on to Tony, but he didn't. J. R. ran into a similar situation, but he did not experience the same consideration from his builder. Instead of repairing an obvious design flaw, the builder tried to explain it away. When that didn't work, he tried to put the blame on his subcontractors; and so it went, until J. R.'s lawyer put an end to the matter by holding a lawsuit over the builder's head until the situation was rectified to J. R.'s satisfaction. After that almost predictable event, J. R. began noticing little quirks in the builder's actions: "The guy was funny: He would use excellent material and employed highly skilled craftsmen to do the job, but he skimped and cheated on the most ridiculous things — like trying to palm off a used light fixture as new. You could look into his eyes and see the greed behind his motives."

The eventual outcome was this: Tony is now in the custom-home-building business as a hands-off partner with his former builder. With Tony's business acumen, an infusion of a million dollars in capital, and his builder's skill and vision, the two have managed to build quite a sizable development company, worth over a hundred million dollars, and they did so in just a few years. J. R., although extremely happy with his new home, has referred more than a dozen of his friends to builders other than the one who built his home. Last I heard, J. R. had invested a large sum of money in a commercial real estate venture, but not with his former builder.

Greed is the kind of thing you can't hide; it shows through in your actions, motives, and words. From the perspective of attracting people to come over to your side, greed is the single biggest barrier — it repels rather than attracts. Your upbringing, education, social status, authority, or bank account size have little to do with your ability to defend yourself against the invasion of greed into your motives. Greed is a natural byproduct of selfishness, and selfishness is, as we have already discovered, a natural, basic drive in all humans. Selfishness and greed are precipitated by what I like to call "the drive to survive." If we allow ourselves to live out on the edge — become overextended, financially, mentally, physically, or spiritually — our natural survival instincts kick in.

Perhaps J. R.'s builder was just temporarily overextended in one or all of these areas, which might account for his apparent self-centered actions. Whatever the cause, the result is the same: self-centeredness and a tendency toward greediness. And the result is missed opportunity. Yielding to our basic instincts for gain will yield only the basics. *You gotta give to get, and the more you give, the more you'll get.* But remember, you will always receive in kind what you give to others. Self-preservation yields self-preservation. If you want love, trust, honesty, and commitment — or even money, for that matter — you have to give it away first, and then it will be returned to you.

Living Debt Free — A Servant Leader's Financial Plan

Servant leaders seem to take a three-step approach to insuring they have an adequate financial base from which to serve. The three steps are: (1) The elimination of debt; (2) the development of a wealth-building budget; and (3) the adoption of the practice of tithing. Let's break them apart and see if we can learn something we can apply to our own situations.

Elimination of Debt

Debt can be an effective tool in business if used responsibly. But an effective, responsible use of debt requires a good working knowledge of finance, and, as Angelo Facciponti pointed out earlier, the average person doesn't possess such a good knowledge of the proper uses of money.

For every ten new businesses that open in a year, statistics show, eight will go belly-up within the next five years — the percentage presently being experienced in the "dot-com" start-ups is even higher. You can trace a good portion of these business failures to an inherent lack of respect for the proper use of debt; the owners simply buried themselves in debt.

There is always a certain amount of risk we assume when we enter into an agreement to borrow money we don't have for the purpose of buying something we can't presently afford — which is exactly what we do when we hand our charge card over to the store clerk.

When we buy on credit, we often pay too much for what we're buying, and we always pay more than we would have had we paid cash in full — as much as 400 percent higher. Too many people forget there is a price to be paid — in the form of interest — for the money we borrow. Economics correspondent Paul Solman reported that, in 1998, the national consumer debt reached an all time high of $1.4 trillion, and just about half of this amount was in credit card debt. The average American is reported to be carrying a balance of $7,000 per credit card at 18.9 percent interest.

Most people only pay the minimum payment due, the majority of which goes directly to pay interest, leaving only a few cents out of every dollar to pay on the principal. If you are one of these people, what this means is that little weekend shopping spree you just took could take as long as forty-three years to pay off! And that's assuming you never charged another thing again.

Using the above example as a reference, the average American will spend $28,845.31 to buy just $7,000 worth of stuff, and considering some of the things we tend to buy, it's doubtful we'll even remember, forty-three years from now, just what it was we bought for all that dough.

Now consider what else you could do with that $250 per month. Let's say you invest the same $250 a month you would have been sending to the credit card company in a certificate of deposit — one of the most conservative types of investment you could make — and did so for the same time period it would take to pay off your original credit debt. You would have earned yourself a cool $829,117. Beginning to get the picture?

A Sound Financial Approach: Developing a Budget

Of the servant leaders I've known over the years, those who have made the greatest impact on the world have had one thing in common — they were all living virtually debt free when their servant vision came to them.

Developing and maintaining a financial budget is not as big a mystery as it may first appear. In fact, a plethora of information — both on-line and off — is available to assist you in getting your financial house in order.

You may want to consider using one of the excellent electronic financial management tools available. The one I use is called Money Matters, developed by financial guru, author, and radio host Larry Burkett (available at www.cfcministry.org). If you are intent on developing a budget the "old-fashioned" way, using a pencil and paper, then you need to get some help. Your public library is an excellent source of information about budgeting and money management techniques. Low-cost budget counseling services that can help you analyze your income and expenses and develop a budget are also available in most communities. Check your Yellow Pages or contact your bank, credit union, or local consumer protection office for information about them. In addition, many community colleges, universities, military bases, credit unions, and housing authorities operate non-profit counseling programs. If you're on-line, I also recommend visiting www.money.com. There you'll find an excellent tutorial that will lead you step-by-step through the budget-making process.

Although there is nothing fun or sexy about making a budget, the good news is, once all of the tedious, up-front work is done, the rest can be quite fun — especially when you see how much progress you're making in achieving your financial objectives.

The Easy out May Be the Least Profitable

Working harder and sacrificing to repay your obligations may not be the easiest way out of debt, it may in fact be the hardest thing you've ever done, but the experience you will gain in the process will be invaluable to your future success. In fact, when my friend Bill refused to declare personal bankruptcy and vowed to pay off all of his bills in full no matter how long it would take, he discovered not only the source of his great personal fortune, but the makings of his servant vision as well.

In the early summer of 1985, Bill was sitting on top of the world. His little company, Hawkeye Pipe Services of Muskogee, Oklahoma, had grown to be one of the oil industry's top manufacturers of drilling pipe. Hawkeye had also become one of the little town's biggest employers, a fact Bill was proud of.

Bill, his wife Kathy, and their two young daughters lived in a beautiful home situated in one of Muskogee's finer neighborhoods. Bill was actively involved in community affairs and enjoyed the admiration of much of the community. By all accounts, he was living the good life.

One bright sunny day in early July, Bill sat across the table from Jay Jones, his "operations chief," with a smile on his face. "Looks pretty good," Jones said glancing at the company's most recent profit statement. "You bet," Bill replied, "the money's flowing in like water and there's no end in sight." Two weeks later the end came.

"It was as if a hand had reached out from ten thousand miles away and turned off the faucet," Bill told me. Bill was speaking of the events of July 25, 1985 — the day OPEC crumbled. An unforeseen shakeup in the powerful international oil cartel sent the price of crude oil plummeting. The resulting shock wave traveled halfway around the world.

Oil drilling in Oklahoma came to a screeching halt, and with it the orders for drilling pipe. Hawkeye's sales that year had been averaging over $1 million per month, right through the end of July. "August sales were exactly zero," Bill vividly recalled. "Hawkeye went bankrupt literally overnight."

No one could have predicted the turn of events that would land such a knockout punch on the chin of the U.S. oil industry. But despite his excellent business prowess, hard work, dogged determination, and last-ditch efforts, Bill lost his company and, along with it, his comfortable way of life.

Bill stood on the factory floor surrounded by the seventy-odd men and women, who were more like family than employees, tears welling in his eyes as he told them the news. "It was the most soul-wrenching experience of my life," he said as we spoke of that ill-fated day. "Nothing in my life was more traumatic than that afternoon." But that was just the beginning.

Bill watched as the assets of Hawkeye Pipe Services were auctioned off to the highest bidder. The meager sums they generated — pennies on the dollar — were not enough to keep Bill from being held personally liable for his now defunct company's debts.

Bill now faced every entrepreneur's worst nightmare. He was entangled in a web of personal guarantees — more than a million dollars worth. Creditors, as a rule, require the owners of small businesses to personally guarantee the repayment of loans extended to their company. If for any reason the company defaults, the company's debt passes to the guarantor, which in this case, was my friend Bill.

He sat with his head in his hands — over a million dollars of unpaid bills hungrily growling at him from across his kitchen table, and not one cent to feed them.

"That's when the fun started. Lawsuits, threatening phone calls at all hours of the day and night from obnoxious bill collectors, all promising unthinkable reprisal if I refused to turn over the family's food money to satisfy the debt. Whenever I confided my dilemma — wanting to pay my bills, but not yet having the means — I was forced to endure an almost predictable retort of personal insults."

And the insults and personal attacks were not reserved exclusively for Bill. No matter who picked up the telephone, the threats were the same. Bill's daughter Jessica, who was only seven years old at the time, was the recipient of one such insulting call. "When my daughter innocently told the caller that her daddy wasn't at home, the man on the other end of the phone snarled: 'Well, you tell that deadbeat father of yours that if he doesn't pay his bill, we're going to repossess his car.'"

What about personal bankruptcy? It's not that Bill was completely unfamiliar with the bankruptcy process. Before he started Hawkeye, Bill was a practicing attorney for a number of years and so had a good understanding of bankruptcy law. But, for Bill, personal bankruptcy was just not an option. Bill was morally opposed to the idea. His sense of honor would not let him rest until all his obligations were paid. "These were people I owed money to. To declare bankruptcy would have been to stiff them. I'd simply have to find a way to repay them."

For comfort, Bill turned to his friends and associates — most of whom were nowhere to be found. "It was like they were all made of smoke on a windy day. People who would frequently drop by my home on a Friday night to play poker or go to the ball game were suddenly avoiding me. It was as if my business failure was somehow contagious, and if they hung out with me, it might rub off on them."

As Bill was flipping through the newspaper one day, he happened upon an unusual ad. The FDIC (Federal Deposit Insurance Corporation) was auctioning off a group of "nonproductive loans" it had inherited from a failed bank in Tulsa.

Bill read the ad and shook his head. "They actually expected someone to throw good money after bad." He tossed the ad into the trash, only to have the ad confront him again the following day. This time he gave it pause before tossing it once again into the trash. It wasn't until the ad beckoned his attention for the third time that he gave it some serious thought. "It was like this ad was appearing in the paper just for me."

Bill contemplated his own plight: He wasn't unwilling to

pay his obligations; he wanted to pay, he just couldn't meet the outlandish demands his creditors were making of him. He wondered: What if there were others like him out there — not "deadbeats," as the bill collectors often referred to him, but honest people who, like him, had fallen on hard times? They would pay when they had the time and means. Maybe these loans aren't "nonproductive" at all...maybe the people trying to collect them are just taking the wrong approach. I could work with these good people and help them find a way to repay what they owed, on a time frame they could handle — and I could help them regain their dignity again.

Bill shared his vision with the only person, outside of his family, he trusted — his former employee Jay. "Jay was one of the few people in town who would still associate with me."

The two men jumped into Bill's truck and headed for Tulsa. Between the two of them, they didn't have the forty cents for the toll road, so they drove the dusty back roads to the site of the auction.

When they got there, they didn't find a crowd: "Only one other guy showed up, and he ended up leaving before the show even started. Three million people read that ad, and Jay and I were the only two guys who even saw an opportunity, or were dumb enough to show."

Bill knew that success in this mission would call for a completely different mind-set. The methods of debt collection employed since the beginning of time had not been productive at all.

In the past, uncollectibles, bad debts, or "charge-offs," as they are called, are assigned to a collection agency. The collection agents, often using whatever tactics they can get away with, attempt to collect the debt. The agency then collects a commission, usually thirty percent, on the debts that it successfully collects. The debts that the agency cannot collect are given up for lost and written off the company's books as a complete loss.

Bill's vision was revolutionary: He would buy the debt outright, for two cents on a dollar; nothing like this had ever been done before. Once he owned the debt, he knew that if they could collect even three cents on a dollar, he would pay for his original investment and walk away with a 50 percent profit. The downside was obvious: he risked not being able to collect a cent, losing everything and plunging deeper into personal debt himself.

Neither Bill nor Jay knew a thing about the collection business. But with the confidence that often accompanies ignorance, they plunged headfirst into the debt pool. There was one problem. They needed $13,000 to put the deal together, and, between them, they didn't have $13. Where were they going to get the money?

I would have loved to see the look on the banker's face that day Bill walked into his office and said: "I know I owe you over a million bucks already. I also know that you know I have no way to repay you just yet. But, I need you to lend me $13,000 more so I can go out and buy some other people's bad debt." There is no reason in this world why this banker should risk $13,000 on a guy who is over a million dollars in debt and has no visible means of support. All logic and reason were against Bill that day, but he walked out of that bank with the money he needed anyway.

Sitting alone at his kitchen table, armed only with a telephone and a newfound empathy for what it was like to have fallen on bad times, Bill collected over $64,000 from that first portfolio of bad loans. To those of you who like round numbers, that's a 400 percent return on his borrowed investment! Bill took the proceeds and plowed the whole amount into an even bigger portfolio. The process continued over and again, with predictable results.

A story published in *INC.* magazine referred to my pal Bill as "one of the richest men in America." Although it is no secret that Bill is one of the few self-made billionaires in the world, I would say his real wealth lies in his unwavering commitment to a vision he never would have volunteered for, yet could not turn away from.

Almost fifteen years to the day later, I talked with Bill about his plans for the future. "So, what's next," I asked. I listened as he gave me his vision for the future. As he spoke, I could hear the unmistakable tone of a servant leader in his voice. As I listened, I got the feeling he was looking into the future through the eyes of God himself.

The mission Bill is living, born out of great personal pain to a man uniquely qualified to handle the difficult challenge, is destined to touch the lives of tens of millions of people who need the guidance of a skilled servant leader such as Bill.

A Servant Leader's Formula for Financial Abundance: Tithing

The development of a servant leader's plan for financial abundance differs from most every other budgeting and financial plan in one critical area: the concept of tithing.

The word "tithe" is an Old English term meaning "one-tenth." So the concept of tithing, in the context of the servant leader's plan for financial abundance, is to *reserve one-tenth of your net available income for use in a particular purpose or purposes.*

The principle of tithing is applied to the servant leader's budget and financial plan in three key areas: (1) the development of a sound financial future; (2) as seed money to fund a servant vision or mission; and (3) to maintain a state of personal balance and stability in an unbalanced and unstable world.

Visionary leaders need to invest in their future, to insure their basic needs will always be adequately provided for. The best way to accomplish this is to include in your budget a provision for what I'll call "self-tithing." To tithe to yourself, you need to reserve the first 10 percent of your take-home pay and place it into an interest-bearing investment vehicle — stocks, bonds, mutual funds, et cetera. By doing this, you allow the money that you have worked for to begin *working for you.*

By investing the first 10 percent of your weekly paycheck, you are assuring a sound financial future for yourself — which is one of the most powerful actions you can take to insure your ability to serve the needs of others.

The next level of tithing is directed toward the funding of a specific vision or mission that you feel strongly about. I call this a "vision tithe."

I have periodically made reference to something I call a servant vision or servant mission — I use the two terms interchangeably. What I am referring to is a compelling drive to champion a particular cause, right a wrong, serve an identifiable need of a particular individual or group, or perhaps even give birth to a new and important industry — the likes of which you would never have taken upon yourself to do.

Although we will be covering this topic in much greater detail in a later chapter, what you need to know about this vision for now is this: part of what you will need to have in order to see this vision through will be money, and since you can never tell when, in how many ways, or in what form this vision will present itself to you, you will need to prepare for its inevitable coming.

You will accomplish this in the same fashion as preparing for a solid financial future — through tithing and investing. Only the investing you will do here will be twofold: First, you will invest the proceeds of your vision tithe in some type of short-term investment vehicle, a money market or mutual fund account. When the time is appropriate, and you are called to do so, you will invest the money that is needed in your servant vision or the mission of another servant leader.

The next level of tithe is what I call the "essential tithe." This tithe is also to be invested — but this time the investment is in you. It is from the proceeds of this tithe that you will have the available funds for: (1) self-improvement and continuing education (to ensure your mental needs are met); (2) a hedge against crisis and emergencies (providing you with peace of mind); and (3) wellness and recreation activities (to ensure you always get the rejuvenation you will need).

Ensuring that you will have enough money when the time comes to pursue a new direction in your life, while being able to support yourself and your family, begins with planning now. To meet the inevitable and often protracted financial obligations of servant leadership, you need to develop a healthy attitude toward money and a patient understanding of the part money will eventually play in the fulfillment of a vision you may not yet see. You need to evaluate your present behaviors and attitudes with respect to money against the model of the "haves" and the "have-nots" — adopting more of the positive, uplifting, wealth-building ones and letting go of the ones that have been holding you down. You need to begin managing your finances using the servant leader's formula of tithing: investing in yourself, your vision, and your future.

Now that we have covered what you'll need to do in order to prepare yourself physically, mentally, spiritually, and financially to identify and serve the needs of others, it's time to take the next step, learning how to put all we have learned into action.

Part III

The Practical Side of Identifying and

Serving the Needs of Others

CHAPTER 11

Who Are You Serving?

From a practical standpoint, identifying and serving the needs of others is a blissful marriage between art and science. When you distill it down to its basic principles, you're left with only three questions:

- Who are you serving?
- What do they need?
- How are you going to get them what they need?

First, Get the People Right

I was having lunch the other day at a wonderful little Indian restaurant near my home. It's the kind of establishment where the whole family plays a part in the business's success: dad cooks, the eldest son cleans and sets the tables, mom runs the cash register, and the youngest daughter — about nine years old — entertains the patrons with her book of crayon drawings. "This is a picture I drew of an alien holding a whoopee cushion." Pretty authentic, I thought; a point I haplessly attempted to convey through a mouthful of curry. "This one's my favorite. It's a picture of the people of the world."

I looked down at her drawing and there were four, costume-draped people — each about the perspective size of the continent of Asia — standing atop a realistic replica of the globe. "That's very nice too," I said, having had time to swallow.

"Yeah, but the people aren't right — they're too big and the world just isn't right either. I'm thinking about entering this picture in an art contest that my brother is holding between me and my friend Patty, but I think I have to redo it — what do you think?"

"I think it's a wonderful picture, but I do think your perspective and relation need to be addressed."

She cocked her head, wrinkled her face, and shouted, "you're silly," as she headed for the back room of the restaurant, swinging her sketchbook as she walked.

By lunch's end the young girl reemerged from the back room with a new version of her favorite picture. She plunked it down on the table for my inspection. "Wow!" I said, "this is very nice" — and it was. She had redrawn the picture, only this time the people were standing on the shore overlooking the ocean, and they were all holding hands; she even had taken the time to include a smiling starfish and a few happy-looking dolphins, and the perspective was perfect.

"Yeah," she replied, "I thought about how to make the picture better — should I change the world, or should I change the people? I decided to work on the people. I figured, once I got the people right the world would get right all by itself."

You know, that nine-year-old may have had a problem with the perspective of a crayon scene, but she has got a tremendous perspective on life.

Once we get the people right, then the world gets right all by itself. If we're going to understand and serve the needs of the people of the world through our unique personal service, what better place to start than by fully and completely understanding the person or group of people we intend to serve? If we get the answer to this question wrong, like so many businesses do, we are doomed to failure.

Let's examine each of these key questions.

Who Are You Serving?

As we've seen, this is the guiding question that will not only define your audience — who you should be focusing your attention on — but it will also serve to keep you out of trouble by reminding you not to let nature take over your decisions and actions. The moment you place your needs above those of another or confuse your needs with theirs, you have let nature take over and you have lost your servant leader focus.

This question is usually straightforward, although you do need to be careful in the beginning not to try to justify your innate predisposition to serve yourself. For example, you might think, "I'm really serving Jane by stealing this account away from her, because she's overworked already and does not need another client to weigh her down."

Or you might be trying to justify some of the decisions you have already committed to without considering if they really are effective solutions for needs other than your own. For instance, suppose you and I really like watching movies. We like watching movies so much that all we want to do all day is sit around surrounded by movies, watching them and talking about watching them. Together we decide that the only way we can accomplish our desire is to quit our respective jobs and open a video rental store, which we do. We sell our cars and mortgage our homes to get the start-up cash needed to buy a plethora of videos and rent a storefront in a local strip mall. Unwittingly, we have fallen into the common "if you build it they will come trap," which is responsible for more business failures than fifty other reasons combined.

If you look at our little scenario, you'll see that we are trying to serve our needs without ever asking whether what we want to do is actually serving anyone else's needs. We have just assumed that since our lives are driven by the desire to watch movies, so are a whole host of other people's. We imagine that the number of people so motivated is so great that it makes no difference that we have just opened the fifteenth video rental shop on the block.

We would have a better shot at success if we were to first determine, with great depth and accuracy, who it is we intend to serve with our video rental shop. If you take an even closer look at the above example, you can catch a glimpse of yet another example in a very long list of unnecessary and perhaps insulting acts, such as offering your comb to a bald man. Just because it works for us does not necessarily mean it will work for others.

Okay, now suppose after trying your best at talking sense to me, I still insist we open our video shop. What will make our plan work? Well, before we give our two weeks' notice and head down the road to video bliss, we need to first find out a little about who our prospective customers might be. This might include how many of them there are, where they live, how many videos these people rent each week, what days of the week they rent videos, what kind of movies these folks like to view, and so forth. Then we need to know what will make these folks stop doing business with the other fourteen video rental shops that are trying to eke out a living and start doing business with us.

A good way to accomplish this is to meet our customers' needs, including those that are presently going unmet, better than any of our competitors. So far, this is a lot of common sense, right? Well, it is. But it is also a lot of hard work. You see, your success is directly proportionate to the depth of understanding you have about the people you intend to serve. The more you know about them, the better. Your goal is to actually get to know more about those you serve, or intend to serve, than they know about themselves.

What Do They Need?

This one's a bit trickier, for a number of reasons:

First, *people don't necessarily know what it is they actually need* because most people are focused more on what they want. In fact, it might be more appropriate to say they focus on what they think they want rather than on what they need to do in order to get what they want. Using myself as an example, I know I want to have a twenty-nine-inch waistline, but I'm not sure how I can get it and still eat ice cream for dessert every night.

Often, once people get *what they say they want, they find it is not what they wanted after all.* I have a friend who has, for as long as I've known her, expressed her desire to move to the West Coast. Two years ago, she picked up her life and followed her dreams, but all she found was a nightmare. Now all she talks about is how much she hates where she lives and how much she misses New York.

Many times what a person says they want is either pure fantasy or a knee-jerk emotional response that masks what they really want and need. My friend Ron Kuby is one of the most brilliant and celebrated trial attorneys in the country. In dealing with his clients, he finds a jagged disparity between what they say they want and what is actually doable or what their true inner expectations really are. Many of his criminal clients, especially the ones who are obviously guilty, want to get off without doing any jail time, which by Ron's account is pure fantasy. In civil cases, clients who have been wronged initially express a strong desire for revenge — "I want the bastard to pay for doing this to me!" — when, according to Ron, they realize later all they really wanted was a simple apology.

To actually determine a person's needs, all you need to do is simply ask questions — a lot of them. Asking questions and listening to what people say, and don't say, in response can go a long way in uncovering a person's real and legitimate needs. We too often stop our inquiry after the first question, How can I help you? This question assumes the other person is aware of his real needs, and this assumption is a trap. People rarely understand their true needs, or if they do, they don't wish to convey them to others. To uncover a set of real needs, we need to continue our inquiry until we uncover the truth. The matrix later in this chapter will help you learn how to do this.

Many times, *people don't know what they really need because they don't know what is available.* Such was the case with just about every great invention ever devised, including electricity, the telephone, the personal computer, and even the wheel. If people have never experienced something — like indoor plumbing, penicillin, or wireless data transmission — they may never know how it can improve the quality of their life. What people need is often hidden because of their limited perspective. It can only be seen by a trained observer with a much broader perspective.

Such was the case that confronted the executives at Agilent Technologies, a Hewlett-Packard spin-off facing a rapidly changing health care system.[1] According to an article in *Fast Company Magazine*, more health care is taking place outside of the hospital than in it. All over the world, health-care delivery

---

[1] Rekha Balu, "Listen Up!" *Fast Company Magazine* (Boston), 34, May 2000, p. 304.

is coming directly to the patient: delivered in the home by skilled home-health-care providers, on the street by paramedics and emergency medical personnel, and in urban and rural clinics by skilled physicians and nurses.

In an attempt to realign its health-care products business with the trends, Agilent had to depart from its usual practice of serving the hospital-based physician and focus more on serving the changing needs of the professionals delivering care in the community.

Agilent's challenge was to develop high-tech medical devices that fit the needs of caregivers with different types and varying levels of medical training, such as home health aides, paramedics, emergency medical technicians, and nurses. To this end, Agilent researchers closely studied those professionals and soon discovered a unique problem. The problem was their inability to hear what was going on inside of their patients — literally.

Because patients were now being treated in environments where ambient sounds and distracting noises were virtually uncontrollable — accident scenes, inside ambulances, helicopters, patients' homes — the practitioner's ability to hear critical clinical sounds was greatly diminished. The stethoscopes these professionals were using were designed over one hundred years ago, and operated, at that time, in a much more controlled environment. The interesting aspect to this whole dilemma was that no one seemed to be asking for a new, or better type, stethoscope.

Although the practitioners themselves were unaware of their real need, the researchers at Agilent realized, because of their broader and more diverse perspective, that the time for a new generation of stethoscopes had come. Agilent responded with an idea for entirely new groups of patient-care devices, employing state-of-the-art technology, rendering the traditional, century-old methods of reading patients' vital signs obsolete.

People often don't know what they need because they lack the perspective to see their own reality, and just as often, because they simply don't know what is available. Since their needs might be unapparent to them, asking them how you can help is useless. To help them, you must first learn about their needs, often by watching them struggle to meet their challenges. Once you identify their needs, you can move on to the equally challenging stage of helping them to meet their needs.

How Are You Going to Get Them What They Need?

Answering this question can be surprisingly tricky. This is due simply to that annoying fact of human nature: *People don't buy what they need; they buy what they want.* So, even though you have just discovered the need for and built a better mousetrap, until you convince the people you've chosen to serve that what you have to offer is going to scratch them where they itch, your prospects for success are dismal.

Like with my friend Ron's legal clients, the first thing you may need to do is reeducate the folks you want to serve about the facts of reality. Ron's advice: "Sometimes you've just got to explain the realities of life to them as plainly and simply as you can. In a case where my client is guilty and still wants to walk away without serving time, I have to say, look you're going to have to go to jail, what we need to do now is work to limit the time you are going to have to serve." Sometimes this approach works, and other times Ron will end up losing a potential client because of it. Either way, he is serving the legitimate needs of his client — by either leading them back to reality or not taking on the clients no attorney can help, thus increasing his ability to serve those clients who really want, and need, his help.

Many times, convincing others they have an unmet need takes nothing more than leading them through a series of questions designed to root them in reality; other times, convincing them takes *proof by example.* Such was the case with the telephone, the electric light, the zipper, and even something as commonplace as the Band-Aid.

Before Earl Dickson's invention took hold, bandaging your own finger was an awkward, contortion-filled feat of physical prowess. You had to unroll a piece of standard surgical gauze and trim it down to size, unroll a strip of adhesive tape and cut off a few inches, then you had to single-handedly wrap the gauze around your finger while trying to keep it sterile, then hold it down and secure it in place with the strip of tape. Not an easy task. In 1920, Earl Dickson changed forever the way we bandage our own boo-boos.

As Johnson & Johnson Company lore has it, Dickson invented the Band-Aid in response to a need demonstrated by his wife Josephine. In her role as a homemaker, Josephine would often nick, cut, abrade, or burn her fingers. Earl, the son of a doctor, often patched up his wife's injuries. Unfortunately, Josephine almost always had to wait until he returned from his job as a cotton buyer at Johnson & Johnson. Both wished for a way Josephine could handle the task of bandaging her own fingers.

One night, Earl sat at the kitchen table in front of a box of surgical gauze, a roll of adhesive tape, a pair of scissors, and a sheet of crinoline (a stiff cloth made of horsehair and linen, usually used as a garment liner). Earl laid out long strips of adhesive tape, sticky side up, on the kitchen table. Next, he cut the surgical gauze into small squares and placed them onto the tape, a few inches apart from one another. Trimming the crinoline to match the width and length of the tape, he covered the pads and sticky portion of the tape, and rolled up the strips.

Now, whenever his wife suffered a kitchen mishap, she could trim off a neat little bandage and apply it to her own finger. The invention worked so well, he brought it to the attention of his bosses at Johnson & Johnson, who also saw merit in the idea. Johnson & Johnson began mass-producing the original hand-made strips in 1921. The public's response was less than enthusiastic, however. It was not until the company began handing out samples, in mass quantity to the kind of folks who could really use them, such as butchers and boy scouts, that the idea finally caught on. Now Band-Aids are the staple in everyone's first-aid kit, and, at last count, the company has produced more than 100 billion of the little suckers.

In order to serve the needs of others we usually use our own resources — physical, mental, spiritual, and financial — as well as our experience, talents, and acquired skills. There are times, however, when the situation calls for more than any one person is capable of giving. This is when we must call on the skills, talents, and resources of others — like the doctor or lawyer who calls in a colleague with specialized knowledge or the business-woman who seeks public funding to expand her business so it can serve even more people. Just as we have a set of unique skills and definable resources, so do others. We need to network with others, tapping into their individual resources to get a big job done, in the same way an organization — like a school, a hospital, a trade association, or company made up of a large number of diverse individuals — serves the needs of its clients, patients, or customers.

The success of the Band-Aid has an inherent commonality with all other "mega-successes," whether or not those successes actually involved the invention of a new gizmo or thingamabob, and that commonality is motive. The motivating power that lies behind the initiation and follow-through of any world-changing development is service to something or someone other than oneself. As long as we concentrate our efforts and attention on identifying and serving the needs of others, we will remain on the road to success and personal fulfillment. As you progress in your abilities and develop a working understanding of the principles of servant leadership, it will become increasingly easier for you to tell when you are on track and when you have once again fallen into the trap of serving yourself. Until then, you can make effective use of the following decision-making matrix. The matrix will guide your thoughts and actions toward the process of identifying and serving the legitimate needs of others, and away from the self-limiting actions of serving yourself. The matrix can be easily adapted to guide an organization as well as an individual servant leader.

The Servant-Centered Decision-Making Matrix

Using the following decision-making matrix will aid you in making better, more servant-based decisions. Before taking any action, answer the following succession of questions as they relate to the action that you are about to take.

By taking the proposed action (describe the action):

Who am I serving?

(Note: If the answer is "me," stop here and rethink your proposal.)

List everything you can about the person or group of people you intend to serve, including but not limited to: age, race, marital status, likes and dislikes, where they live, where they tend to hang out, what they do for a living, where they work, how they get from place to place, what they value, et cetera. Remember, the more you know about them, the better able you'll be to identify and address their legitimate needs. By legitimate needs, I mean things, actions, or situations that will make the person or group stronger and more independent, and thus better able to serve others' needs or achieve a positive desire.

What are the legitimate needs of the person or group you intend to serve?

1.

2.

3.

4.

5.

The legitimate needs of a person or group can be determined through:

• skilled observation;

• asking open-ended questions about their dreams, aspirations and challenges (open-ended questions are those questions that require more than a "yes or no" response, e.g. What is your idea of a dream job? or Can you tell me some of the things that you believe are holding you back? or even, If you could change one thing about [blank] what would it be?), then looking for similar and common responses; and

• determining a person's legitimate desires (those desires

that are positive, productive, and legitimately obtainable), and what will be needed to achieve them.

Now, identify the unmet needs of the person or group. A helpful way to uncover a person's unmet needs is to delve into their pet peeves: What really ticks them off? What stresses them out? Where do their inconveniences and challenges lie?

*Describe how, specifically, your proposed
action serves each of the needs outlined above:*

*Describe how your proposed action
serves your organization's needs:*

*(This section is intended for evaluation of the actions of an organiza-
tion in pursuit of meeting its clients' needs.)*

Describe your proposed plan to meet the needs you have identified:

What skills, resources, and specialized knowledge
will you need to carry out this plan?

1.

2.

3.

4.

5.

What skills and resources will you need to acquire from others?
(List here what you need and from whom you intend to obtain it.)

1.

2.

3.

4.

5.

The strongest part of this matrix is asking questions at EVERY STEP. This habit, of asking questions at every step, may get you into trouble now and then, but it just might lead you to your life's goal.

Why Ask Why?

Wouldn't it be safe to say human beings are born to be curious creatures? After all, what is the first question a child learns to ask? It's the question "Why," right? So, if we are born to be naturally curious, why do so many people lose their curiosity as they grow into adulthood? That reminds me of another question: Why do you suppose croutons come in airtight packages? Aren't they just stale pieces of bread to begin with?

I'm not an expert on the subject, but wouldn't it be safe to assume our upbringing might have had something to do with our growing reluctance to ask questions as we got older?

Thinking back to your childhood, what type of response did asking questions usually get you? It was typically a negative one, right? We were always admonished by someone older than us when we asked too many questions, weren't we? Which brings up a question I've been carrying around with me since childhood: Why is it such a positive thing to be a *wise man*, but so negative to be a *wise guy?*

It's kind of silly to discourage a young child from being

curious about life, wouldn't you agree? Isn't being naturally curious a good trait to foster in our children? Shouldn't curiosity be a trait we respect in each other as well? Isn't our natural search for answers to the world's questions the basis for just about every discovery we can think of? Why do you suppose, then, most people you meet — including many so-called scientists, yield to society's pressure to stop asking questions? It doesn't make sense, does it? I'd say something's *out of whack*, wouldn't you? This brings up my next question: Why do you suppose, when something is broken, we say it is out of whack? Does that mean then, when it is functioning properly, it's *whacked?*

Wouldn't we be better served as a society if we fostered a heightened degree of curiosity in our selves and others? And if we did, wouldn't we then be less likely to think we need to have all of the answers? Wouldn't that then lead to us being more open minded about things we don't understand like: Why do screws always come packed in odd number quantities, when we use them in even number quantities, or, why do you suppose they post pictures of criminals on post office walls? Is it to get us to write to them? Wouldn't it make more sense to print criminal's pictures on postage stamps — so the postmen can look for them while they are delivering the mail?

Have you ever restrained yourself from asking a question, for fear you'd look foolish doing so? Isn't it really more foolish to appear as if we know the answer, rather than to learn what the correct answer really is? Wouldn't it be wonderful if we could rid ourselves of such a self-limiting need?

If a method existed that would systematically eliminate your conditioned reluctance to ask questions for fear of appearing ignorant, would you be curious as to what it is? Do you think you might benefit from such a method? Do you think such a method would open up new vistas of learning to you?

Well, why then don't we examine a simple, yet effective method we can apply to our own life to get us into the habit of nurturing our own inquisitiveness?

There is a method of gaining an unlimited flow of knowledge that is used effectively by most every professional you can name — lawyers, doctors, analysts, plumbers, mechanics, police officers and pollsters just to name a few. Do you have any idea what this method might be? The method dates back to Socrates; in fact, it is commonly known as the Socratic method for obtaining knowledge. All you need to do to master it is to begin asking why about everything, and doing it all of the time. And, it's really fun to do.

In fact, you might have noticed I've been having a little fun of my own since the beginning of this chapter. Take a look back and see how many questions I have posed to you in the past few minutes. Once you get the hang of it, you can turn entire conversations into nothing but a series of questions.

Why would we want to go through life like a giant question mark? For a number of reasons: First, it is the only way we can ever be effective as servant leaders — we can only serve the needs of others if we take the time and spend the energy to learn what their actual needs are, not assume we know. I've found over my history, some of the most injurious blunders I have ever made were the direct result of having made an assumption about a person, thing, or situation — that predictably proved to be totally off base. By constantly asking questions, we eliminate the potential of making false assumptions.

Next, when we make it a practice to ask the question *why* about everything, and do so all of the time, we become immune to hucksters and con men. Shysters swindle us by appealing to our vain desire not to appear foolish. We can disarm any con artist simply by asking too many questions.

And finally, from a purely vainglorious standpoint, asking questions serves to make us more likable to others, and also makes us appear more intelligent. The reasons for this are simple: when we ask a person questions, and do so in a sincere and earnest manner, we direct the spotlight of attention on them and not on ourselves. All people like to feel important, and when we seek their wisdom, their level of importance is elevated in the process. In turn, we end up making a far more favorable impression on someone than we would have if we had tried to impress him or her with our knowledge on the subject.

To be most effective as a servant leader, we need to develop, not suppress our natural curiosity about all things.

A Gymnasium for the Mind

In addition to expanding our natural curiosity for all things, we need to expand our experiences, skills, and knowledge base as well. It's far too easy to fall into a comfortable routine when it comes to most things in life. For some reason — I guess it stems from our human desire to *fit in* with the crowd — we live our lives from the center of the road, not wanting to appear too extreme in one way or another.

My friend Phil manages a steakhouse. Phil tells me that an overwhelming majority of his customers order their steaks to be served *medium*. It is my guess these same people serve up large chunks of their life in quite the same manner. I often wonder if it's no coincidence that the word *medium* rhymes with the word *tedium*.

Servant leaders, to be effective, need to take a bite out of life from all sides — not just from the middle. Servant leaders require a broad-based knowledge that touches all the extremes of points of view and points of life. When we get caught up in living a routine, our minds become lazy. We end up living our lives more by rote than by experience.

It's my guess you took the same route into work today that you have taken since you began your job. As a result, I bet there are times you can't even remember making the trip, yet you know that you must have because you are already at work. The problem with living our lives on autopilot, is that we become numb to the wonders of the journey — we miss more of our lives than we experience.

Our mental muscles, like the muscles of our body, tend to atrophy when they are not used — we need exercise our intellect in order to keep it healthy and strong. To provide for this, we need to build a sort of mental gymnasium out of life routine. By incorporating these practices into your daily routine, you can improve the fitness of your mind without giving the matter a second thought.

Learn something new, at least once every year. Set aside a nugget of time in your annual schedule with which to learn something you did not know before — take a course in anthropology, learn to build a piece of furniture, learn a new language, learn to play the bassoon.

A good place to start is with things that you are interested in, but have never had the opportunity to learn. Next, move on to things you are mildly interested in, but would not have otherwise pursued. Finally, get involved in learning something you have no interest at all in. This method keeps you from inhabiting the same mental plane all of your life.

Learning by doing is a lot more exciting than learning by reading, plus learning by doing forces you to interact with a whole new group of people you normally would have never met.

For those of us who are social introverts, the prospect of meeting and associating with a new and different group of strangers usually makes the little hairs on the back of the neck stand at attention, but from a great deal of personal experience I can tell you this: I have never once regretted the experience — as uncomfortable as it was in the beginning.

Please understand, you are not necessarily seeking this new knowledge for the purpose of becoming an expert on the subject — although you just may happen upon something you want to make a regular part of your life, as was the case when I took a course in stained glass making, studied voice-over artistry, and learned to fly a plane.

For instance, just because I learned how to fly, does not mean I plan to become a professional pilot. I simply learned for the experience and understanding, and ended up having a great deal of fun as a benefit. The fact is, you may never use the knowledge you gain in your present career, but I assure you, the experience will not go to waste.

My first speaking engagement resulted from my learning to fly. I met the executive who would later hire me while on an instructor-mandated cross-country trip. My flight instructor and I shared a crowded lunch table with the woman at an airport luncheonette five hundred miles from my home. After years of dealing with the study of servant leadership and the strange happenings that seem to surround it, I have learned there are no such things as coincidence in this world. I can honestly say, if I had not learned to fly, you would not be reading these words today.

Life Lessons from Another Comedy Giant

Question the ridiculous in your behavior and in that of others. Comedian Groucho Marx was a guy who possessed an innate ability to make us laugh at the ridiculousness of our behavior.

I recently had lunch with a fellow who was a writer on the

1950s game show, "You Bet Your Life," hosted by none other than Groucho Marx. The writer said it always felt like a waste of time to write jokes for Groucho; his observations and resultant ad-libs were far more hilarious than any team of comedy writers could ever have developed.

During our visit, he regaled me with one such incident: In the course of interviewing a particular female contestant, Groucho learned the woman had twenty-two children. Groucho then asked the obvious question: "Why?"

In response, the woman sheepishly said: "Well Groucho, I love my husband."

Without missing a beat, Groucho replied: "Lady, I love my cigar too, but I still manage to take it out of my mouth every now and then."

We often can't recognize the ridiculousness in our own behavior. And because we can't, we lose sight of the real reasons we do the things we do, or miss entirely the juxtapositions between our words and our actions. For example, I have a friend who always talks about his desire to live in a house in the country, usually as we sit together on the balcony of his penthouse apartment.

Left unrecognized, these blind spots can cause us to continue living a life that is in direct opposition to our inner wishes. This mental/physical incongruity often works to cause us spiritual unrest.

Like Groucho, we need to develop a healthy, non-threatening way of pointing out the ridiculousness in our behavior and in the behavior of others.

Asking May Lead to Unexpected Riches

In essence, make it a point to expand your field of view and personal point of reference. Your heightened sense of curiosity can turn out to be your greatest asset in the future. It was for Percy Spencer.

His may not be a household name, but I assure you, our households would not be quite the same if not for his special brand of curiosity. The next time you nuke that plate of leftovers, you just might want to pay homage to the servant leader who, out of his need to explain the obvious, was single-handedly responsible for developing the microwave oven.

During his thirty-nine years with the Raytheon Company, Percy Spencer patented 120 inventions, not bad for a guy who never finished grammar school. This self-educated electrical engineer could easily be called one of the greatest inventive minds in the history of early electronics — thanks, in no small part, to his insatiable search for knowledge and his desire to serve the needs off others.

When German bombs were decimating England during the battle of Britain in 1940, it was Spencer who would dedicate his inventive talents to develop a more functional version of the British radar system. His efforts resulted in an ability to increase radar tube production from seventeen per week to twenty-six hundred per day. His labors not only earned him recognition in the form of the Distinguished Service Medal (the United States Navy's highest civilian honor), but, more importantly, saved the lives of tens of thousands of innocent human beings — giving them early warning of an impending attack.

Not long after World War II, Spencer was walking through one of his laboratories at Raytheon. When he stopped in front of a magnetron unit (the power tube at the heart of a radar set), he suddenly noticed the candy bar in his shirt pocket beginning to melt. Most other scientists might have chalked the occurrence up to coincidence or the expected effect of body heat on chocolate, but not Spencer.

Spencer approached the incident in the only consistent manner he had come to know — he ran out and bought a can of popping corn. Holding a dish of kernels in front of the radar unit, Spencer watched in excitement as they began to explode. The experiments did not stop there. The next morning Spencer brought in a teakettle from home, cut a viewing hole in the each side, placed a chicken egg in the kettle and the kettle next to the magnetron. I believe the resulting explosion was the first documented case of a scientist with egg on his face. Raytheon funded and patented the device in 1953, and Percy Spencer was credited with the invention of the first microwave oven.

Before I conclude this chapter, I have one more question for you to ponder: How fast would lightning really be, if it didn't zigzag?

CHAPTER 13

If Love Is Blind, Why Is Lingerie So Popular?

One of the reasons I've based the last two chapters of this book on the importance of asking questions is because we need to realize that many of the things that we've blindly accepted as truth ain't necessarily so. We take too much for granted, including "givens" that are derived from old adages like "love is blind." When we do, we accept what is on the surface as being the true answer and thus miss the real, underlying answer. Think of how unhappy we men would be if the creators of Victoria's Secret had believed that silly adage, love is blind.

Uncovering the Hidden Needs of Others through Observation

Beauty may run skin deep, but our legitimate needs tend to run a whole lot deeper. Asking well-formed questions and listening intently to the answers, as we discovered in the last chapter, can reveal a lot about a person's perception of their challenges, needs, and wants. But this is typically only the first step in uncovering a broader, more fundamental set of needs.

To get to the core of a person's legitimate needs, we must look past the surface. We must look past their outward expression in words of what they perceive their needs to be, and toward what their actions tell us about them and their true needs.

People don't necessarily know what their real needs are. Why? Why isn't eleven pronounced "onety-one"? I have no idea. All I know is, if you ask people what it is they need, the answer you receive will most likely be a reflection of what they want, rather than what they need. My guess is people may never know what they really need because they don't know what is available or possible. It's up to the servant leader to help them identify and uncover their real needs.

Recall the lesson we learned in the story of the uniform shop and the little boy. The customer in that story would have said she was looking for a particular type of uniform if she had been asked by the salesperson, when what her *legitimate* need was to have someone occupy her child while she shopped for what she wanted. Not until the clerk actually observed the customer in the act of trying to shop with her son in tow, and did so through the eyes of a servant leader, could the customer's real need be discovered.

If we take the time to ask the appropriate questions, listen intently to the answers, and then compare what we hear with what we observe, we may discover the real needs that lie hidden below the surface. And when we do so, we can forever alter the course of civilization, or at the very least have an impact on the quality of life of those we serve and all those who are touched by them.

People's legitimate needs may not always be apparent at first glance. Just like the precious minerals that lie below the earth's surface, sometimes you have to dig a bit in order to uncover them, but the rewards you realize will always be worth your efforts. The best tool to accomplish this type of *educated* digging is our own unique set of life experiences. When we look at a problem through the spectacles of our own experience, we tend to see solutions that nobody else can see.

Only when we uncover and address the legitimate needs of others can we expect a mutual win: The other person wins because her real needs have been met, thus allowing her to get what she wants, and we win through the rewards of our efforts. Such was the case with Whitcomb L. Judson, the fellow who invented the zipper. Judson, a mechanical engineer, invented the first zipper as a shoe fastener, because he had grown tired of the tedious task of fastening the many hooks and eyes required to keep his boots in place.

The problem with Whitcomb's invention was that it was unique — nothing even remotely like it had ever existed before. This can pose quite a problem, because as long as people don't know they need something, they are not going to be interested in it. You may be able to see an unmet need in other folks, but until you convince them that you can scratch them where they itch, you're going nowhere, which is exactly where Whitcomb's first company was headed. In 1906, the company was struggling just to pay its bills.

After perfecting his original design, Whitcomb and company (actually called the Hookless Fastener Company) were faced with creating a demand for a product nobody even knew they needed. Just like the customer in the uniform shop who had never had anyone occupy her child while she shopped, experience was the key. Unless and until a person experiences the benefit of a new and different solution, they will often be blind to the benefits they might receive if they opt for that solution. Oddly enough, World War I was the catalyst for the proliferation of the zipper. Once the zipper got into the hands of the soldiers, there was no stopping the demand for more. By 1930, even in a world gripped by the greatest economic depression of recorded history, the company was selling more than 150 million zippers a year.

I Know Something You Don't Know!

Your unique life experience is often all that you'll need to identify a common need that no one else has been able to see. Although he was only a "kid" at the time, software pioneer Bill Gates was able to identify a widespread need that was obvious to him but not obvious to the seasoned executives at IBM, nor even to the "inventors" of the personal computer, Steve Jobs and Steve Wozniak.

When Gates arrived on the scene, the burgeoning personal computer industry had zeroed in on the computer itself. Executives at Apple and IBM were locked in a heated race at the time for market dominance in the manufacture and distribution of personal computers. As a software engineer, Gates's unique perspective enabled him to see a common need overlooked by both Apple and IBM.

Through personal experience, Gates realized that by itself the personal computer was useless. Without a set of instructions to tell the computer what to do and how to do it, the product that rolled off the assembly line was, at best, nothing more than a curious new electronic gizmo that whirred and hummed and displayed symbols on a television screen — and at worst, a thirty-pound, putty-colored paperweight.

Gates and company, under the newly adopted moniker Microsoft, responded to this common, yet previously unidentified need by offering what it called a "disk operating system" (DOS).

The new MS-DOS (Microsoft Disk Operating System) was

simply a collection of short programs, or "routines," that enabled the computer system and user to manage information; but as Gates and company saw it, it was the most integral part of the future of personal and business computing applications.

So little thought was given to the need for an operating system that the founders of Apple were said to have summarily dismissed Gates's sales pitch before he even began. The executives at the helm of the business goliath IBM, at the time, weren't much better when it came to seeing the potential value of a great idea.

Everyone was so busy bathing in the selfish afterglow of scientific achievement and grabbing at his or her respective slice of the computer-market pie, that they were blinded to the obvious problem at hand. Perhaps if they had looked, they would have seen that the key to widespread public acceptance, a.k.a. a clamoring horde of money-wielding patrons eagerly queuing up to buy a new personal computer, was dependent on meeting a critical need of the buyer. That *need* was the computer's ability to do things for them that they *actually needed it to do*. Selfishness, as you can see from the the above example, can cause our vision to be blurred, and blurred vision can be costly.

Blurred vision, resulting from a bad case of the *what's-in-it-for-me syndrome* on the part of IBM executives, led to what has become known as the largest business blunder in history. IBM's failure to secure exclusive rights to the original disk operating system, by either purchase or an exclusive licensing arrangement, allowed Microsoft to sell the original disk operating system it had developed for IBM to any other company that had the money to pay for it.

Although IBM literally "invented" the personal computer, they would almost immediately relinquish their market dominance to the unending flow of competitors who would clone the hardware technology and purchase the essential operating system (at a much lower price, incidentally) from Microsoft. Conversely, because Gates and Microsoft were the first to identify and respond to a basic, widespread need, they would quickly take their places in history. Funny, in my research I never could find out the names of the IBM people who made that fateful decision.

As was the case with the zipper and the disk operating system, sometimes our own needs are a clue to a greater common need. Often, if it hurts us, it just may hurt others who are in the same position. If this is the case, and we work to solve a common problem, we can end up turning competitors into customers.

Don't Compete, Create!

I first met Ted when he waltzed, uninvited, into my new business office and plunked a slick brochure on the table in front of me. The masthead on the pamphlet was printed in an eye-popping yellow against a black background; it read, "A business without signs is a sign of no business." As he slid the brochure across the table to be certain I could clearly read it, he looked me straight in the eye and boldly said, "I see I got here just in time."

Ted was a sign painter and was as talented as he was proud of what he did. Ted loved painting signs. A third-generation "signsman," as he often referred to himself, I guess you could say sign painting was in his blood. Ted was as skilled in salesmanship as he was in sign painting. Over the next few years, we would do thousands of dollars of business together, not counting the dozens of customers I referred to him. His prices were fair and his product was good, plus he always seemed to have an uncanny handle on what kind of signs our business seemed to need. You can imagine, then, my dismay when Ted came into my office one day and announced he was moving his business out of state. Ted would be hard to replace.

In response to his growing dislike for city life, Ted moved his family to a remote area of the North Carolina coast. He settled in a small seaport town one hundred miles and two-and-a-half hours from the nearest "big city," which, by Ted's reckoning, was "not big at all."

Ted had not even gotten his family settled in their new home when he began to set up shop in a small, vacant building near the center of the boat-building district. Once the shop was ready for business, Ted set out on a hunting expedition for new customers. From business to business he went, introducing himself and his new sign-painting service to the merchants and business people of the small town. But it seemed like everywhere Ted went, he received mixed signals. He was welcomed warmly, but the same story always followed: "I've got nothing for you."

There were already five sign painters in the same town, and it seemed as if they already had most of the good accounts all wrapped up. Ted is not the type of person to be easily discouraged, however. He turned over every stone in that small town, as well as those within a thirty-mile radius. He managed to drum up some work — enough to eke out a meager living — but not nearly enough to raise a family of six.

It was beginning to look as if the only two professions in the whole three-county area were fisherman and sign painter. To make matters worse, when Ted did get a job, he had to travel over a hundred miles on old country roads in order to get the supplies he needed.

About eighteen months passed, and the business was still only trickling in. There was just too much competition for the little area to support. One day on the five-hour round-trip to the supply store, Ted got an idea: why not turn the competition into customers? Ted figured that if he had to make the trek to the supply store, so did his competitors. Why not use his years of expertise to help his competitors instead of competing with them.

Ted returned home and began work immediately. He transformed his workshop into a sign-painter's supply house, and he did so in a big way. Over the years, Ted's main source of irritation came from having to deal with supply houses that were run by people who knew little or nothing about running a sign business. They were never able to give him advice about the advantages and disadvantages surrounding the use of the various materials that were available, because they themselves had never had any firsthand experience with their use. This resulted in a lot of costly trial-and-error experimentation. This would all change under Ted's direction.

The sign-painting community met the new shop with great enthusiasm. Ted stocked a huge and diverse line of materials at the ready. His new venture was an instant success. Over the years, Ted has added customers to his business by utilizing direct-mail advertising, a toll-free number, and recently a Web site.

Now sign painters from all over the country benefit from Ted's years of experience and first-hand knowledge. All because Ted used his unique experience to discover a common need and then worked to fill it.

Yahoo!

The same kind of intuitive vision that motivated my sign-painter friend Ted to begin serving the needs of others was behind the creation of the Yahoo! Internet search engine. Jerry Yang and David Filo, while still electrical engineering students at Stanford University, devised a method of categorizing the vast amount of information available over the Internet. The project sprang out of the pair's habitual addiction to surfing the World Wide Web, an activity it's been reported, they spent more time with than on their respective dissertations in computer science. Within a year of its inception, demand for their service reached such network-jamming proportions that they were forced to move their operations off campus to larger computers located at Netscape Communications in Mountain View, California. The company went public in early 1996, and, unlike most Internet start-ups, the company began to make money quickly and has been growing ever since.

When speaking of his first meeting with Yang and Filo, Yahoo! president and CEO Tim Koogle said, "What struck me immediately was that they had filled a fundamental need and had done it intuitively. That's what you look for in starting a business."[1]

We've seen that a legitimate need can be something that is obvious to someone with a particular set of life experiences, as was the case with software pioneer Bill Gates, and we've seen how it is possible to uncover a common need in pursuit of a need of our own, as witnessed by my friend Ted, the sign painter, and the founders of Yahoo! Some needs, though, can be more than just one level thick; there are instances where a surface need can be detected, and if you look a bit deeper you can also detect its systemic cause. By looking at each level independently, it is possible to uncover more than just one set of needs, in which case you will effectively reap more than just one set of rewards. Early detection of a hidden need at the systemic level can also help keep you from getting caught up in it altogether. Take for instance the case of the disappearing nurses.

---

[1] Stanford University's School of Engineering Web site.

The Case of the Disappearing Nurses

In June of 2000, the American Medical Association announced a severe deficit in the number of nurses in the United States, and pronounced a grave prognosis for the future of health care because of it. The AMA estimates that by the year 2020, the demand of the health-care system will exceed the pool of available nurses by over 20 percent. This translates to cancelled surgeries, postponed medical procedures, and longer, lonelier waits on the bedpan for a lot of future hospital goers.

The news of the shortage did not come as a surprise to Trisha, operations director for a New Jersey–based home-health-care agency. "We saw the swellings of this tsunami about a decade ago. Home-health agencies like ours have always had to compete for qualified nurses with hospitals, nursing homes, long-term care facilities, schools, and with industry."

In the late 1980s and early 1990s, the hospital and nursing-home industry's answer to the shrinking pool of nurses was to simply throw money at the problem, increasing nurses' salaries — simply passing the costs along to the insurance companies, which were paying the bills.

"Home-care agencies have never had that option; most of our clients pay for services out of their own pockets. There's a limit to what we can charge for our services; if the price goes too high, everybody suffers. Our solutions had to be much more creative."

So how did her agency respond? "We first looked at the initial problem. We had to turn away patients because our staff of five hundred was too small to handle the increasing demand for our services. That's not a great scenario. The hardest thing I have ever had to do in my life was to turn away the tired, stressed-out family of a sick or dying person in the middle of the night because I did not have a nurse or home-health aide to send to them, and

I was having to do just that with increasing frequency."

The managers at the agency took a closer look at the problem. They were losing a growing number of skilled caregivers, not to hospitals, nursing homes, or other home-care agencies, but to motherhood. Although statistics are beginning to change a bit, women preponderate in the nursing profession by 95 percent. Younger women were taking professional hiatuses to raise a family, and those whose children were old enough to be left on their own were staying away. Mom's nursing skills had become dull and outdated from the years she spent away from her quickly evolving profession. Fear of reentering the workforce was keeping many nurses away.

Looking Past the Obvious

The managers began looking at the obvious set of needs from a different angle, their own role in the equation. They began by identifying the people they as managers should actually be serving. In the past, managers thought of themselves as an extension of the agency, serving the agency's mission, which was to serve patients. As they reexamined the problem, they realized that the needs they should really be addressing were those of the organization's nursing staff. If the managers did a better job at identifying and meeting the legitimate needs of the nurses, they in turn could do a much better job of meeting the needs of their patients. After all, the managers were not the ones delivering patient care. The managers figured if they could help the nurse in the field to better meet her own needs, that nurse in turn would be stronger and more able to serve the needs of the patients under the agency's care.

"That was the turning point — from there it was a piece of cake." The agency mounted a fact-finding campaign, including getting to know their best workers on a much deeper, more personal level. What challenges did they face both at home and at work? What were their fears, dreams, and aspirations? What did they feel was getting in the way of their desires? It worked like a charm. "It was the first time anybody ever asked them questions like the ones we did. We learned what they really needed from us, which was nothing like what we thought they needed. From there we worked together at making it happen."

Today Trisha's agency enjoys one of the lowest turnover rates in the industry; and recruitment of top professionals is no longer a problem. "We now have second-generation nurses in our little family — sons and daughters of our employees are coming to work with us, some even before they graduate — as apprentices. Our agency has gained a reputation for caring about the people who care for those in need, and the ones who have really benefited in the process are our patients and their families — and that's what it's all about in the first place, isn't it?"

Looking past the obvious for a deeper set of needs can have rewarding financial outcomes, too. This certainly was true for the woman who captured the title of being America's first black female millionaire, whose story I'll tell you in a later chapter.

I'll close this chapter with this advice: Dare to look past the obvious, for it is there that you might catch a glimpse of how you can serve the unmet needs of others. Use your own unique experiences, trials, and pain to breathe purpose into your vision. Next, set your mind to developing a mission, a dream of how you can help others to meet their needs, and when you dream, dream big dreams. Ask God for guidance in making those dreams a reality, and then take immediate action on your plan, because if you don't, chances are those dreams will die from neglect. "The tragedy of man" said Dr. Albert Schweitzer, "is what dies inside himself while he still lives."

CHAPTER 14

If We Are Here to Serve Others, What Are Others Here For?

We can learn a lot about how to serve others by watching how others serve us — or fail to serve us. We can often pick out events in which someone acted in ways that comforted our soul, put our mind at ease, got us over a critical hump, guided us in the right direction, or in some other way aided us in our struggle with life. We can also find a host of examples of what we wish would have happened, but for some reason did not. If we take the time to carefully analyze how others treat us, or how we wish others would have treated us in the past, we can develop an effective benchmark for how we can serve the needs of others.

We all need to feel loved and appreciated. We all need to believe that those who are in a position of power over us actually have our best interests at heart. Perhaps the best way to continue your quest for the hidden needs of others is by learning to identify ways in which other servant leaders have worked to serve your needs and those common to all people. To this end, I present to you another story, about the life of another servant leader I once knew. Let's see if, together, we can learn a few things about purposeful living from his example.

Lessons I Learned from My Best Friend

It was September 24 — a Thursday. I was out of town on a weeklong business trip. I was enjoying lunch with a client and his wife. I ordered the grilled chicken salad. Midway through my salad, a piece of chicken seemed to lodge itself in my throat. I drank an entire glass of water trying to get the thing down, to no avail. I was breathing fine, so I didn't panic, but I was very uncomfortable. The feeling passed eventually, and I had completely forgotten about the incident until a few days later, when it happened again. The episodes became more frequent. A few months later, the pains in my stomach started.

The month of January saw me doubled over in pain on a hotel floor, while the "blizzard of the century" howled just outside my window. I was worried. The lump in my throat seemed ever present, the pains in my stomach were more frequent, and the intensity of each exacerbation grew more severe with the setting of each day's sun. The only time I was not bothered by the symptoms, it seemed, was when I was on the speaker's platform or working with a client. But the very moment I was alone in my room...whomp, there it was.

I had not confided to anyone about the pain. I just didn't want to worry anyone, especially my family. I thought it would go away — eventually. In the back of my mind, I had an idea of what the symptoms could mean.

When I was a boy, my father died from stomach cancer. He had the same symptoms. To make matters worse, my paternal grandfather's life ended in the same manner. His illness, as I recall, also started with these symptoms.

Memories of my father's last year on earth were rekindled.

I recalled how I watched helplessly as he suffered, unable to eat solid food or swallow a sip of water, receiving all his sustenance through an eight-inch-long rubber gastric tube protruding from his abdomen.

I thought about my symptoms. Was I the next in line to suffer this fate? It was time for me to seek medical attention. Well, to be more accurate, the time to seek medical attention had come long before — let's just say I was finally ready to make the call. I sat in the doctor's waiting room, nervously flipping through a two-year-old copy of *Time Magazine*. I got up from my chair and crossed the length of the waiting room so I could examine the diplomas hanging on the wall.

Why do we do that — check out the doctor's diplomas, I mean? Is it to assure ourselves that the person who will soon be peering at us from the opposite end of some ominous-looking diagnostic contraption — as we lie there in that famous knee-to-chest position on the cold examination table, our dignity exposed for all to see — actually has a license to do that sort of thing?

If you really think about it, it doesn't make much sense. You can't tell from the wall decorations what kind of doctor he or she is. No, for that you should always examine the doctor's office plants.

The office nurse caught me reading the doctor's credentials. She was nice about it. She just smiled and said "The doctor will see you now." Holding the door to the inner office open with her left foot, she extended her right arm, pointing the way down the hall.

A quick glance over my shoulder at the brass-potted, variegated holly bush that lived in the far-right corner of his waiting room told me it was okay to enter.

I was ushered into a ten-foot-square examination room,

handed a white, short-sleeved, knee-length, linen robe with a full split up the back, and told to undress and "wait in the room for the doctor." Did I have a choice? After all, where was I going dressed in that getup?

After what seemed to be an eternity, the doctor entered the room without comment. He spent a few moments silently flipping through the four-page questionnaire I had filled out.

The only dialog that took place between the two of us was a battery of one-sided questions and answers — him asking the questions and me giving the answers — regarding the circumstances and symptoms that had brought me into his office. When the *interrogation* was through, the *punishment* began.

I'll spare you the graphic details of the hour-long examination. Let's just say the good doctor saw more of the "inner me" that day than I thought was humanly possible. The examination ended as abruptly as it had begun. As he exited the room, he handed me a stack of papers and directed me to the hospital for more tests. I paid the bill and left.

It took me about an hour to wind my way through the unmarked maze of the hospital corridors to the X-ray department. When I finally arrived, I was told to take a seat in the waiting room and I would be called when *they* were ready for me. I amused myself by pondering who *they* were. Quickly bored, I wandered over to the magazine rack in search of something to occupy my thoughts. I picked up another copy of the same two-year-old *Time Magazine* that was in my doctor's office and finished reading the article I had started earlier that morning.

I heard my name being announced over the waiting-room loudspeaker. I guess the mysterious "they" must be ready for me. I was directed into a dimly lit room that felt more like a refrigerator than a hospital examination room. Once again, I was told to undress and put on another well-ventilated robe in place of my nice warm clothes. I thought, What gives with these robes? Are they some type of uniform that serves to distinguish the inmates from their captors? I took off all of my clothes and put on the robe, but I kept my socks on — partly out of rebellion and partly to keep my toes from getting frostbite on the cold, hard floor.

Since no one had taken the time to inform me what type of tests I was supposed to undergo, or what those procedures involved, I amused myself by looking around the room at the various contraptions and paraphernalia that dangled from them. I tried to surmise what each was used for and which would be used to torture — oops, sorry — I meant to say *examine* me.

By now, the subzero temperature of the room was causing my nose to run and my fingers to turn a lovely shade of blue, and the air-conditioner vent was blowing cold air right at my exposed behind. Throwing dignity to the wind, I ventured out into the corridor in search of someone who might be able to fetch me a blanket, or snow parka, to keep from freezing to death. Oddly enough, I did not draw that much attention from curious onlookers. In fact, I met a number of other inmates, dressed in the same uniform that I was wearing, who informed me there were no blankets to be found, but if you kept moving, you would eventually begin to feel the sensation returning to your legs. "They" eventually found me wandering the halls and returned me to my cell — I mean *room*.

The doctor — well, at least I think he was the doctor; he never did introduce himself — entered the room and began the procedure without comment, save of course an occasional command like "move to the left" or "hold your breath." The technician signaled the examination's end by pausing in the doorway long enough to say "You can put on your clothes and go now."

I drove home feeling more worried than ever.

As my car pulled into the driveway, I saw my dog Dryfus —
a hundred-pound, four-year-old German shepherd — playing
in the yard. "That dog loves to play," I thought, as I watched
him running and jumping for joy.

My mind flashed back to the day my wife and I picked him
out of the litter. Dryfus was the last one out of the pen. When
all the other puppies saw him, they scattered. As soon as he was
free, he ran and jumped and bit the behinds of his brothers and
sisters. I knew he was special from the first moment we met.

Two months after we got him, he once again proved to be
something special. He became a source of comfort for me during that eighteen-week bout with drug-resistant pneumonia.
Dryfus never left my side, and his presence proved to me the
healing power of animals. He ran and jumped with exuberance,
his massive frame rippling with muscles. I often saw him pick
up a fallen branch of oak, ten feet long, and trot around with it
in his mouth like it was a Popsicle stick. He had an unyielding
zest for life. You would never know by looking at him that he
was dying of cancer.

The following Tuesday I was sitting in my office when the
voice on the intercom informed me that my stomach doctor was
on the line and wanted to speak with me. The verdict is in, I
thought, as I lifted the receiver with trepidation.

I listened nervously as the good doctor informed me of my
fate. "Based on your test results and the facts I gained from my
detailed examination of your gastrointestinal system," he said,
with a painfully slow cadence, "I have arrived at a diagnosis for
your condition."

"And…and," I asked anxiously. "Well," he continued, "I
feel that you are suffering from the effects of globus hystericus."

Globus hystericus, my God, this sounds serious, I thought

as I dropped the phone. I leapt from my chair, ran across the room, and reached for my copy of *Dorland's Pocket Medical Dictionary*. *Globus hystericus*, it explained, was a "subjective sensation of a lump in the throat" — a hysterical reaction to stress that manifested itself as a choking feeling.

A wave of relief washed over my entire body. "I'm not dying!" I happily exclaimed aloud, "I'm just a neurotic!" My assistant rushed into my office to see what all the yelling was about. I repeated my statement. She rolled her eyes, shook her head, and exited without saying a word.

My dog Dryfus's illness, coupled with the sudden death of a friend, had started a chain reaction of worry in my life: I had already lost one friend, and I was about to lose another. My real worry came from having to face the inevitable, and along with it a moral dilemma. All my life I have been morally and philosophically opposed to euthanasia. I could not bring myself to put my best friend to death. Yet, how could I cause this helpless animal to suffer for the sake of my beliefs? The worry I was feeling was actually causing the choking feeling in my throat and the pains in my stomach.

I later discovered, while leafing through my *Webster's Dictionary of Word Origins*, that the word "worry" is derived from an Old English word that means "to choke."

Now, I'm not a psychiatrist, I don't even play one on TV. So I figured I had better enlist the help of an expert and see if he couldn't help me gain an understanding of this whole thing. I called my friend William, a professor of psychiatry and a practicing psychiatrist, but I thought he might be able to figure out what was wrong with me anyway.

William confirmed my suspicions. He told me that, although I had no major problems in my life, I was apparently consumed by worry and it was manifesting itself as the sensation of a lump in my throat. My symptoms were real all right, but they were caused by the negative use of my imagination. I had become a victim of my own thoughts. The good doctor's prescription was as follows: *start focusing your attention on helping other people who are worse off than you.*

It all began to make sense. First, the appearance of the symptoms seemed to coincide with the troubling events of the recent past. Second, I was only free of the symptoms when I was involved in something that directed my mind away from me and toward someone or something else. When I speak to an audience or consult with a client, my focus has to be 100 percent on them and 0 percent on me. Speaking, consulting, and writing became my safe harbors. For the next four years, I battled the effects of worry on my mind and my body by throwing myself into my work. It took that long, but it worked.

I learned a lot about the benefits of turning my attention to the needs of others from my best friend Dryfus. No matter how much pain he was in, he always focused his attention on us. He never gave up his relentless vigil over our home or his family. He never stopped bringing joy to everyone he met or allowed you to see the pain he suffered.

Doctor Rogers Fred III was Dryfus's oncologist. I bet you didn't know there were veterinary oncologists. Well, there are. And Rogers Fred is, hands down, one of the best there is. I have been hanging around the medical professions most all my life, but I have never met a practitioner with such focus, compassion, and dedication as Rogers.

My introduction to the workings of the veterinary profession came at a time when I could freshly compare the differences between how vets served their patients (and families) and how "human" doctors and medical professionals had treated their patient (me!). One of the jagged disparities I noted was the level of genuine caring exhibited by vets and their staff compared to the doctors, nurses, and technicians I had just encountered. Dr. Fred and his staff absolutely loved what they were doing — you could tell that by the way they worked with Dryfus. You can learn a lot about a person by watching him or her at work, and as I watched these servant leaders at work, I learned volumes. Their sense of compassion and commitment to excellence was instantly evident to both man and beast.

Another stark difference between doctors of veterinary medicine and their counterparts who treat two-legged animals is the veterinarian's willingness to show emotion to both their patients and their clients. You can't feign affection or compassion to an animal; they see right through it. This compassion has been "trained out" of medical practitioners who treat humans.

Medical and nursing schools the world over have taught students that they must never get too close to their patients. The term used to describe this behavior is "detached concern." I often wonder how effective a parent, lover, friend, or family member you or I would be if we practiced "detached concern" in our personal lives.

In almost every interaction I had with the medical community during my stint with that globus thing, I felt as if I were invisible. If the people who were treating me acknowledged me at all, they did so as if I were a bother rather than the primary reason for their being there. Vets and their staff constantly talk to and reassure their patients, even if their patients can't actually "talk" back to them. I saw a lot of laughing and smiling going on during the course of my visits, and I also saw real expressions of sorrow, grief, and consolation when a patient died.

Our society has only recently acknowledged the therapeutic effects of touch and love in human medicine. In many ways, modern medicine lags far behind veterinary medicine. My wife and I were never kept in the dark about the many tests or treatments our dog Dryfus was going to receive, nor were we kept blindly waiting for test results without knowing about how long the process would take. We were informed and comforted every step of the way.

I learned a great deal about serving the unspoken needs of others from Dryfus's caretakers, but the one from whom I learned the most was their patient. Thirteen months and two weeks into Dryfus's treatment, we sat in Dr. Fred's office as he explained treatment options. Dryfus was no longer responding to chemotherapy. His condition was worsening each day, but, as his doctors often said, "you could never tell by looking at him."

As we talked, I looked over at Dryfus and he looked back at me with such intensity in his eyes: it was as if he was trying to say, "Are you people nuts — what are you trying to accomplish here? Face it, it's over, now let's play some ball while we still have the time."

He must have been in excruciating pain — the cancer was ravaging his young body. The decision I had been avoiding and agonizing over for thirteen months was staring me in the face. We agreed to wait a week and see what could be done.

The next day when I returned from work, Dryfus met me at the door as he always did — a bright yellow tennis ball in his mouth. He was ready to play, and play we did. He ran through the yard like a pup, jumping and catching his ball. We played until well after dark, and he ended our play session with one of his famous "flying hugs." His heart was filled with joy. Both our hearts were filled with joy. We hugged for what seemed like forever, neither one of us wanting to let go, both somehow knowing this special time would be our last.

Twenty-seven hours later, at 11:03 P.M. on a rainy, cold

November night, Dryfus died. The entry in my journal reads: "I just lost my best friend."

My wife was heartbroken. I was heartbroken. All who knew him were heartbroken. His life touched many people, as did his passing. As people will often do, in order to help heal the wounds left by the passing of a loved one, we reminisced about the times we shared and the many rewarding friendships that were spawned because of his life, friendships that would live on long after him. He gave all of himself, with all his heart and all his soul, to the very end.

Could it be possible that even an animal is capable of servant leadership? Looking at his life and the richness he brought to so many others, there is no doubt in my mind what the answer is.

The globus thing and the stomach pains went away once I learned what I had to learn: when we focus attention on ourselves instead of on others, we choke the magic from our lives. But when we choose to serve others in the only ways we know how, we enrich the lives of everyone, ourselves included. And when we give, without expectation, we reap far more than we sow, and our love lives on forever. These lessons I learned from my best friend.

Part IV

Miracles in the Making

CHAPTER 15

Like Moths to a Flame

The information contained in this final part of *Never Offer Your Comb to a Bald Man* was perhaps the most difficult piece I have ever written. The reason for this is simple: Although I have personally lived and experienced many of the phenomena I will attempt to describe to you here, I'm still not sure I fully understand them myself. In an attempt to broaden my descriptions, I have consulted with many others who have experienced much of the same strange goings on and have included their thoughts with my own; but still much of what I cover in this chapter is not as explainable as I wish it were. If I were forced to classify in terms we all might be able to relate to, I would have to label many of the events and accounts in the following material as *miraculous*. I hope you understand and forgive many of the vagaries.

From time to time I have made mention of something I've come to know as the "servant vision." The servant vision can best be described as a driving force that leads a person to walk a specific path, toward an end even that person might not be sure of — yet, for some reason, there is no doubt it is the path they must walk.

The Servant Vision

One characteristic I have been able to associate with the servant vision is that the vision appears as if from nowhere, but the servant leader somehow knows it is being directed at him or her.

Think back to my story of my friend Bill, who was deep in debt and who later made another fortune as a bill collector. If you remember, Bill's vision came to him in the form of a newspaper ad. Bill recalls: "It's like the ad was there just for me," a feeling that would later be confirmed at the auction: "Over three million people read that same advertisement; I was the only one who showed up."

For my friend Curtis Sliwa, founder of the world-famous Guardian Angels, a red-beret-sporting, five-thousand-member all-volunteer public-safety brigade known for protecting the welfare of citizens from the ravages of crime, Curtis's vision came in the form of the fearful and hopeless faces of his friends and neighbors, and in the sights of crime-ridden, decaying neighborhoods they once called home.

For my friend Ron Kuby, social activist and famous criminal trial attorney, the vision came wearing the mask of social, racial, and legal injustice.

Physician Maria Montessori, founder of the Montessori system of education, saw her servant vision in the faces of the children who were labeled as hopeless and discarded by their parents and society like yesterday's trash.

The servant vision came to Moe Howard, servant leader of the Three Stooges, in the healing and joyous sounds of laughter, and to classical musician Evelyn Glennie in the silence.

The servant vision fell from the sky with the bombs of

World War II for electrical engineer Percy Spencer, and rose up from hell for John Walsh, host of "America's Most Wanted."

For me, the vision came on a lonely stretch of road with such a force as to push my car to the side of the road so that I could write out the words to a mysterious and cryptic poem, which had buried in its words the formula for the makings of a servant leader.

The vision often comes in the form of personal pain and human suffering, as it did for Dr. Viktor Frankl — and for a woman the world has come to know as Madame C. J. Walker.

Black Gold

Legend has it Madame C. J. Walker made her fortune by inventing a line of hair-care products, including a hair tonic she dubbed Madame Walker's Wonderful Hair Grower. If we take a closer look, however, I believe it's easy to see that her overwhelming financial success was derived not from the sale of cosmetics, but rather from a lifelong commitment to serving the needs of others.

Born Sarah Breedlove on December 23, 1867, in Delta, Louisiana, the firstborn daughter to slave parents, her servant character would be honed by poverty and molded by adversity. At the tender age of seven, fate saw her sitting helplessly by, watching as a yellow fever epidemic took both her parents. Young Sarah was left alone and charged with the care of her two young siblings.

By age eleven, in an attempt to better her lot, she and her sister, with only the clothes on their backs, moved to Vicksburg, Mississippi, where the girls took in dirty laundry to make a living.

At age fourteen, Sarah married Moses McWilliams. One year later, she became a mother, and two years after that Moses was killed in an accident, leaving Sarah alone with her baby.

Sarah knew that, if she and her young child were to make it, they needed to move to a place that offered better opportunities, so she mustered the courage to move her family to St. Louis. There, she found work as a washerwoman. The long, hard days stacked one atop another, and the harsh lye soap took its toll on Sarah's skin. But nothing seemed to detract this servant leader from her objective. As Sarah worked into the night to earn a living, she dreamed of one day being able to educate her daughter and elevate her from a life of poverty.

From the start, Sarah's life was etched by the mark of a servant leader and she found comfort and joy going to the aid of others. A newspaper article told the account of one such an incident: "She [Sarah] read in the [St. Louis] *Post-Dispatch*...of an aged colored man with a blind sister and an invalid wife depending on him for support. Without acquaintance of any kind with the family, she went among friends in behalf of the distressed people, succeeding in collecting $3.60, which she gave to them. She felt it was her duty to do even more [so] she arranged for a pound party through which means groceries in abundance were given."[1]

As Sarah became more familiar with a number of St. Louis's prominent black women, she noticed a difference between her physical appearance and theirs. The hair on the heads of the women of affluence was full and healthy looking. In contrast, her own hair was broken and patchy, revealing her bare scalp in many places. Sarah's hair was no different than the hair of countless poor black women of her time. Like many other servant leaders, Sarah developed a keen sense of intuition that enabled her to see past the situation. Sarah knew, from personal experience, how great a role a woman's personal appearance has

---

[1] Bundles, A'Lelia Perry, *On Her Own Ground: The Life and Times of Madame C. J. Walker*, (New York: Scribner, 2001).

in how she sees herself. She also knew the limitations a poor self-image can have on a person's ability to rise above circumstance and create a better life. Sarah knew if she could change the way poor black women saw themselves, that change might very well be the beginning of their climb out of poverty. But the mission that had chosen Sarah was far bigger than anything she could ever have imagined.

Like many servant leaders, Sarah prayed for guidance. She later told a reporter: "God answered my prayer, for one night I had a dream, and in that dream, a big black man appeared to me and told me what to mix up for my hair. Some of the remedy was grown in Africa, but I sent for it, mixed it, put it on my scalp, and in a few weeks my hair was coming in faster than it had ever fallen out."

If the tonic worked for Sarah, perhaps it would work for others like her, and if that were the case, she could only imagine the countless number of women whose fragile self-esteem would be benefited.

Through more prayer, Sarah discovered that the help she needed to fulfill her vision was located in another part of the country. Once again, powered by the blind faith of the servant leader, Sarah gathered up her life and moved to Denver, Colorado.

Once in Denver, Sarah became a clerk in a drugstore, the perfect venue to begin working on her dream. Under the tutelage of her employer, she learned much about chemical compounding. Sarah applied that knowledge during the evening hours after the shop was closed, perfecting her hair-care formulas. With no formal training in chemistry, Sarah developed formulas that would serve many other women. Likewise, Sarah never formally studied psychology, but her years of observing and serving others made her a brilliant analyst of womankind.

She knew how difficult it could be to change a person's self-image. The women that Sarah was committed to serve had grown accustomed to viewing themselves through poverty. This made it hard for them to see the need for a change in their outward appearance. If her products were to do what she intended them to do, Sarah had to go straight to them.

Without wasting a minute, she developed an in-home demonstration program — the first of its kind — and began taking her new products door-to-door. She demonstrated her products directly on the hair of her prospective clients, and she did so free of charge. After shampooing their hair with her Vegetable Shampoo, she applied Wonderful Hair Grower to their scalps and then a fine dressing of her special oil, designed to smooth and finish the hair.

Seeing the amazing transformation in their once-tattered appearance was all these inwardly beautiful women needed to boost their confidence. Denver's black women responded by buying her products with eagerness.

Fate led Sarah to get back in touch with an old friend, Mr. C. J. Walker from St. Louis. Before long, they were courting and Walker soon proposed marriage. Sarah began referring to herself in the advertisements as "Madame C. J. Walker," both as a means of distinguishing herself as a married woman and, as lore has it, to convey to her product line a Parisian influence.

In no time the little company was earning profits of $10 per week. Despite objections from her husband, friends, and family — who warned her of certain failure — Sarah took her show on the road. After a year and a half, Madam C. J. Walker was netting over $35 per week — which at the time was more than twice the wage of the average white male worker and over twenty times that of the average black woman worker.

From all accounts, it was at this juncture when Sarah's servant mission really kicked in, leading her to take a series of actions that resulted in the transformation from poverty to plenty for tens of thousands of black women. Sarah began training agents to use and sell her products in return for a share in the profits. By 1908, she had signed on dozens of representatives, and her personal income soared to a record $400 per month.

According to Walker biographer and great-great-grand-daughter A'Lelia Perry Bundles, Madam C. J. Walker received many letters of gratitude, including one that read: "You have opened up a trade for hundreds of colored women to make an honest and profitable living where they make as much in one week as a month's salary would bring from any other position that a colored woman can secure."

Once they can observe their vision unfolding, servant leaders experience enhanced sagacity and the scope of their mission begins to expand. This was the case with Madam Walker.

The Vision Expands As the Mission Expands

By 1916, Sarah Walker and her daughter relocated to Harlem. A wave of black southern migrants was reaching its peak in New York, and Harlem was alive and bustling with activity. The pair's 136th-Street residence also served as home for Lelia College, which at the time graduated over twenty Walker hair culturists every six weeks. Business was at an all-time high, and earnings topped the charts at over $2,000 per week. Like a monument to the rewards of servant leadership, the dream home Sarah built, called Villa Lewaro, still stands tall on the northern banks of New York's Hudson River.

At the time of her death in 1919, Walker's company employed over twenty-five thousand black women, who sold a full line of Walker products door-to-door. If this marketing plan sounds familiar — it should. It is the same concept that Mary

Kay Ash and the Avon Corporation used to propel their organizations to success. Yet, there is an important historical note to consider: Mary Kay did not employ these techniques until 1963, and, although the predecessor of the Avon Corporation (California Perfume Company) was formed in 1886, they did not enlist their army of "Avon Ladies" until 1950. C. J. Walker was truly a servant on the cutting edge of change, and a woman far ahead of her times.

As a servant leader, Walker never forgot her roots or her obligation to serve. Raised in poverty, she shared her immense wealth with the needy. Deprived of a childhood education, she developed and supported institutions of higher learning. And, through her mission and leadership, brought thousands out of poverty through education and inspiration.

The Walker Method of hair care had more to do with developing people than it did with the sale of hair-care products and the beauty education. The program taught black women how to develop their natural beauty and celebrate their uniqueness. As a result, the self-esteem of the students improved and their confidence in themselves blossomed.

Through her legacy, Walker still encourages generations of young people to serve their fellow men and women. "I promoted myself," she would tell audiences. "I had to make my own living and my own opportunity. But I made it! *Don't sit down and wait for the opportunities to come. Get up and make them!*"

The Turning Point

The realization described above is what Juanell Teague, author of *The Zig Ziglar Difference* (New York: Berkley Inspirational, 1999), calls the "turning point nudge." Juanell, a noted authority on the effect turning points can have in our lives, says that these subtle "nudges" are extremely brief periods

— lasting only about one to three minutes. Due to the mental clutter we carry around with us, the majority of the time we rarely get the message — let alone respond. Consequently, Juanell warns, "if you fail to act, these promptings will diminish, and you will miss a life-changing opportunity. But if you act," she reminds us, "you will receive untold blessings."

The servant vision is so strong it often pulls you away from a familiar life path and onto one that is completely different. An odd thing about this path is it defies all reason and logic; it is certainly not of your own design.

For instance, if, fifteen years ago, you had told me, a social introvert of painful proportions, that I'd be leaving a highly lucrative business career to stand on a platform and talk to a room full of strangers about what it means to be a visionary leader, and then devote five years of my life to research and write a book on the subject; I would have advised you to lie down and wait for the drugs to wear off.

The pull of the servant vision was so strong it caused Dr. Maria Montessori to leave her post as Italy's first woman physician and devote her life to something she had absolutely no knowledge of.

Maria Montessori made history the day she reached her hand out to receive her medical doctor's degree; she was the first woman in Italy to do so. Little did she know that, a mere five years later, she would quit the practice of medicine and once again make an indelible mark on the face of history.

As an assistant physician at the university psychiatric clinic, Maria witnessed an unending parade of examples of the frailties of humanity and the cruelties and injustices of society. The ones that kept her from sleeping at night were those that affected the children, especially those who were shunned by society for their failure to thrive in a normal way.

Maria began to develop a deep love for these small, helpless creatures. It was in the faces of these unfortunate children that Maria Montessori found her servant vision.

In 1899, Dr. Maria Montessori left the practice of medicine and became director of the State Orthophrenic School of Rome for mentally retarded children. So successful were her practices that she began to apply the same methods to the education of "normal" children. The result was the establishment of Casa dei Bambini, the first Montessori school for children, which she opened in a ghetto of Rome in late 1907.

Dr. Montessori's methods were very radical for their time. They emphasized the development of a child's initiative, senses, and muscle training by a means of specially designed games and teaching materials that stressed freedom in the child's environ-ment. Montessori's innovations made her a target for many a rotten tomato hurled at her from the hordes of "established experts" in the field of pedagogy. The harsh criticism seemed only to push her forward.

In 1917 Maria opened the famed Montessori Institute in Barcelona, followed by similar training academies in London, other cities in Italy, and the Netherlands. Her teaching meth-ods revolutionized the field of education. There is little doubt that Maria Montessori faced obstacles and personal hardships in the realization of her childhood dream to become a doctor. Her story serves as an example of the obstacle-crushing forti-tude a human being develops once he or she has adopted a per-sonal goal and begins the process of fulfilling the needs that lie between conception and realization. I've always found it amus-ing, that the world doesn't know the Montessori name for this remarkable woman's gender-breaking attainment as Italy's first woman physician. Rather, it is for the contributions Maria Montessori made, once she adopted her servant vision, that pushed her onto the road less traveled, away from goals directed at herself and toward those of a much greater scope. She revolutionized the educational system, not because she was an "established expert" in the field of education, but because she was simply following her unique servant vision.

We often need to leave what is comfortable and familiar to discover what is our true destiny.

The servant vision, in addition to pulling oneself into unfamiliar ground, is also one that:

- will not let you rest — it nags you
- is usually the most illogical, irrational choice of all
- is not something you would have chosen for yourself, and that is how you know it is from God and not from you
- is so bizarre people warn you not to do it
- may come out of pain, personal tragedy, or crisis.

Look once again at the story of my friend Bill, and you will see a perfect example of what I mean by the servant vision. Suppose for a moment it was you standing in Bill's shoes, a million dollars in debt, no job, no prospects of income on the horizon, in jeopardy of losing your home, your car, your good name, and possibly even your family. You fear answering the door and the phone for the risk of another confrontation over money that you don't have. You have nowhere to hide. Insults and ridicule are being hurled your way from every direction. Your friends are avoiding you. Your self-esteem is lower than it has ever been in your life. Would you ever, in your right mind, have conceived of solving your problems by going further into debt, buying the bad debts of other people with the hopes that they would pay you back the money they actually owed to someone else?

The truth is this kind of borderline insanity could only have made sense to Bill, and only after he had gone through what he did.

The path that the servant vision often leads you down is the most difficult of all to follow; it's the path of most resistance, the path least likely to be chosen. The fact is, people naturally seek in life the path of least resistance, the most comfortable, well-lighted, well-traveled, "safest" routes. These are not the routes of the servant leader, and they would not have worked for my friend Bill. If you look at the path Bill took to seize his vision, you might see a decision one breath short of insanity. To Bill, it was the only and obvious choice. Bill did not realize it at the time, but he was preparing to walk the path he chose all of his life. His unique, God-given talents and life skills made him perfectly suited to walk the path that was presented to him.

The Price of Taking Action

No matter what you do for a living, identifying and serving the needs of others is much harder than serving your own needs. You may need to make sacrifices or change your point of view, and often you may be required to place the needs of another above your own. You have to learn new skills, develop and expand your base of knowledge, curtail your spending habits, reduce your consumption of pizza, chili dogs, and beer. You might even have to start being nice to people you used to despise. If you choose to do all of these things, and adopt the headdress of a servant leader, you will no doubt significantly change your lifestyle for the better. If, however, you choose to go one step further by putting aside your human need to design your own ways of serving the needs of others and adopt a vision that you know in your heart and soul is not of this earth, you can possibly change the course of human history. But the investment you will be required to make will be far more significant.

Working with servant leaders over the years, I have witnessed the emergence of a specific pattern of events in each of their lives: A vision appears to them as if from nowhere, they respond to the calling, they take action — very often without any kind of formal plan — and then their world comes unhinged.

I'm really not sure why taking the first step seems to set off a chain reaction of predictably bizarre events: the servant leader's world turns upside down and inside out, all of their usual support mechanisms start working against them, obstacles and setbacks of epic proportions rise from the ground under their feet, as if to knock them off balance. As one servant leader appropriately put it, "It felt like the gates of hell opened up and all that was evil came out to meet me."

Servant leader and Guardian Angels' chief Curtis Sliwa lost two marriages to the pursuit of his servant vision, and his commitment to take on "the mob" almost cost him his life when he was shot five times while riding in the back of a New York City taxicab. It was not as if he got any support from the power mavens of the city his organization of volunteers was sworn to protect; the mayor and police department labeled him a lunatic vigilante — the cops and the criminals hated him equally.

The normal criticism that meets any new idea takes on a more virulent tone when it is directed at a servant leader who is in pursuit of his or her vision. The attacks become more vocal and far more personal, until it's like being, as another servant leader I know once put it, "a mechanical duck in a carnival shooting gallery."

The California artist Thomas Kinkade knows firsthand how nasty the criticism can get. Art critics have all dismissed his work as "vacuous, slick commercialism...aimed at the lowest common denominator of artistic taste."

Known as "the painter of light," Kinkade has built a massive public following for his repertoire of trademark images that bear such names as "Pools of Serenity," "Stairway to Paradise,"

"Wind of the Spirit," and "Bridge of Faith." "The critics may not endorse me," he once declared to a *New York Times* reporter, "but I own the hearts of the people." Based on the $250 million buyers of his art paid in 1999, I'd say he was right.

Thomas Kinkade makes it no secret as to where he feels the inspiration for his unique style of art originates. He once told *People Magazine*'s Russell Scott Smith, he considered "God [to be] his art agent." Why does Kinkade continue to paint despite all of the negative criticism surrounding him and his work? "I paint scenes that serve as places of refuge for battle-weary people," and, he told Smith, "My paintings provide hope to people in despair, provide a reminder of the beauty of God's creation despite the darkness surrounding our lives." And Kinkade knows something about the darkness.

Kinkade discovered his servant vision while painting scenery for the Hollywood film *Fire and Ice* (1982). The pursuit of his vision forced him to leave his full-time job, making it necessary for his wife Nannette — Kinkade's childhood sweetheart — to assume the role of primary breadwinner, working as a nurse on the night shift. Kinkade refers to the period following his commitment to serve his adopted vision as the most difficult period of his life.

Kinkade, like all other servant leaders I know, found that those closest to him were often his greatest detractors. Another servant leader I know once said: "My best friends and family couldn't have been more obstructive and hurtful if there had been a prize for them!"

One thing remains predictable when a person takes that first step to serve his or her servant vision. I think it was best described in the words of yet another servant leader: "Everything in my life that was once as solid as a rock, turned to quicksand over night."

Yet, for some inexplicable reason, most servant leaders press on. Armed with only their rock-solid resolve to keep them going, they put one foot in front of the other and walk steadily on, through the darkness of setbacks, problems, sacrifices, and personal tragedies.

When their darkest moment besets them, they spit in the face of adversity and refuse to quit, and at that very moment, without exception, they report feeling the clouds part and a ray of hope shine through. It's as if they have just passed through some invisible threshold that separated joy from sadness, pain from pleasure, hope from despair, success from failure, the miraculous from the mundane.

Almost at once, all the lights turn green and the road ahead becomes clear and level, and what only can be termed as "miraculous happenings" begin to occur.

Strangers begin showing up to help them — some pointing the way, some with a pat on the back, and still others who come to lighten the load. Obstacles begin to give way, leaving opportunities in their place. Small rewards begin to come to them, like crumbs dropped by another who is leading the way.

Soon, the path of the servant leader begins to intersect with those of other servant leaders, each in pursuit of his or her own vision and each able to lend unique talents, resources, and experience at a moment in time that could easily be termed "perfect."

A servant leader I know describes these people who show up to help us just when we need them most as the "angels who walk among us." I have come to term them something a bit less grand — the "servant leader's network."

It's eerie how they show up in your life and in what form — like the tollbooth attendant who declared, "I have a feeling you're gonna do something special today," the morning of the day I received a telephone call from my editor, informing me this book had been unanimously accepted for publication.

Although I have my suspicions, I have no concrete proof of where these people are sent from or even if they themselves are actually aware of the fact that they have been sent to help. In fact, I can't really speak with any certainty about any of the particulars surrounding the appearance of the network. But I have been able to compile a list of pointers for your use in dealing with the members of this network when they do appear.

Working with the Servant Leader's Network

First, anticipate that the servant network seems to show up according to a time frame that is not the same as yours. Trust in the fact that members of this network will appear just when they should.

Understand, too, that they may come in unusual forms. Those who have come into my life have typically been strangers. Some servant leaders, like my dog Dryfus and his protégé Cosmo, have not been human at all; still, they have taught me more about the art of serving than any human teacher I have ever known.

One of the reasons you were instructed to develop relationships with people who are different from you is because the servant who can help you most often shows up as someone you would never have associated with — someone who usually possesses some views and beliefs you might even have once found offensive had it not been for your newfound tolerance toward people and ideas.

But don't go out actively looking for people to help you in your cause. The people you find in this manner are often not there to help at all, and many may be there to hurt. In this respect, networking, from a servant leader's standpoint, is quite opposite from the traditional businessperson's ideas of networking — standing at the end of your cousin's wedding reception line, handing out business cards to the guests who pass by in procession. The help you need will always come to you, but, at the same time, you can't just sit around doing nothing but waiting for help to arrive.

Like Moths to a Flame

My research on Moe Howard showed me that the pieces of Moe's servant vision continued to fall into place, regardless of the obstacles. For the first few years of their comedy careers, Moe and Shemp performed their stooge act with Moe's boyhood friend Ted Healy playing the straight man. During a road trip to Chicago, Ted, Moe, and Shemp walked into a nightclub called the Rainbow Gardens. On the stage was an odd-looking man dressed in a tuxedo. He was playing a violin, telling jokes, and dancing a Russian dance. They were impressed by his humor and asked him to join the act. The man was Larry Fine, a concert violinist turned comedian.

The new act was an instant hit and Larry replaced Ted as the third stooge; and, as it turned out, just in time. Not long after Larry joined the act, Ted suffered injuries that eventually resulted in his death. For the next seven years the trio enjoyed great success, but midway into the seventh year, the act nearly came to an abrupt end again. When Shemp received an offer to do some "serious" acting, the men put their heads together and decided to include Moe's baby brother Jerome in the act. Although Jerome had no real training as an actor, he did have a knack for making people laugh and was one of the most sincerely kind and caring people the men knew.

Brother Jerome soon joined the act, but there was one problem — his hair. Larry Fine's persona called for him to sport a wild, shoulder-length hairdo, and Moe had already adopted his legendary bowl-on-the-head haircut. Jerome's hair was dark and wavy, in stark contrast to that of his two zany counterparts. Shortly after their first planning session, Jerome returned sporting his new hairstyle — a shaved head. From that point on, Jerome would forever be known as "Curly." The new trio, dubbed "The Three Stooges," was simply magic. So much so, that in 1934 Columbia Pictures signed them to a film contract.

One of the common occurrences servant leaders speak of is the existence of a palpable force that seems bent on pushing them away from continuing their quest to bring goodness to the world. Often, as their work grows in scope and size, and more goodness is spread through the world, this dissuading force seems to grow in its intensity. As one servant leader I know put it, "I felt like I was climbing a mountain. The higher I climbed, the more difficult and rocky the path became, and just as I had the summit in sight, it seemed like the gates of hell opened up and all that was evil joined forces in an attempt to knock me down." It seems like the Stooges had to tangle with the some of same demons that have confronted other servant leaders in their quest to serve the world.

By 1946, the Stooges, all aligned on a single mission, were enjoying a bountiful run of successes, including a number of feature films. They were bringing the gift of laughter to a world that couldn't get enough. Then the unimaginable happened.

It was May 14, 1946. The Stooges were on the set finishing *Half-Wit's Holiday*. The soundstage was sweltering. Curly sat in director Jules White's chair waiting to be called for the last scene. When the director called for Curly to begin his scene, Curly didn't answer. Moe walked out to get him and found his brother slumped in the chair, his head resting on his chest.

"Babe!" Moe cried — a nickname Moe had given his baby

brother as a child. Moe ran to his brother's side. Curly looked up at him but was unable to speak. His mouth was distorted, one side of his face drooped, and tears poured from his eyes.

"I thought my heart would break," Moe later wrote of the emotions he felt. "I immediately knew he had had a stroke. I put my arms around him and kissed him on the cheek and forehead."

Curly Howard, the world's most-beloved Stooge, had fallen. It looked like this would be the end of the Three Stooges. After all, who could take Curly's place? Not only was he a genius in his field, he was kind and considerate and loved by everyone he came in contact with — on screen and off. The public loved him, his coworkers loved him, and his partners loved him. He could never be replaced.

Moe, by now the lead Stooge, needed time to collect his thoughts. Curly required expensive medical care for the rest of his life. Although the Stooges were a success, the studio made millions and the trio received very little financial compensation.

It is in times of crisis that a servant leader's traits, determination, talents, and mission seem most aligned. Their innate drive to aid someone in need gives them the ability to foster an almost superhuman courage and inspires them to develop creative solutions to otherwise insurmountable problems.

Larry and Moe were determined to continue the Stooge's act so Curly could get the medical care he needed. But who was capable of replacing Curly? Finally, the answer came — Shemp! Why not Shemp? After all, he had been the original third Stooge. It took some smooth sales talk, but eventually Columbia bought the idea, and the original trio was performing once again.

Curly's health continued to deteriorate. He suffered several more strokes over the next six years, until, at the age of forty-nine, he peacefully slipped away. Brothers Shemp and Moe and dear friend Larry were heartbroken. But their original driving purpose — to bring the healing power of laughter to the world — moved them on to the next summit.

November 23, 1955, started out like any other day. Moe and his wife Helen were abroad on a long-awaited European cruise. Shemp spent the afternoon at the horse races and then decided to attend an evening prizefight with friends. That night, on the way home, Shemp was sitting in the backseat of the car, telling jokes and laughing with his friends, when suddenly he became quiet. With a smile in his eyes, a cigar between his lips, and the love of life in his heart, Shemp died.

Moe received the news by cable that night. He was devastated. The shock of losing yet another brother was just too much for him to bear; all he wanted to do was give up. Moe's wife Helen and partner Larry knew how much his mission meant to him, so they did what they could to urge him to go on, but Moe seemed to be at the end of the road. Moe finally did muster his courage to go on, but this time it took a lot longer to rebound.

On January 1, 1956, Moe and Larry once again invited a third Stooge into the act — Joe Besser. The new trio produced sixteen short films, but the magic just wasn't there any more. Columbia refused to renew the Three Stooges contract. When Joe Besser left the troop, yet another third Stooge — a comedy performer by the name of Joe DeRita replaced him. The new act opened at the Holiday Inn in Bakersfield, California, and it bombed. Out on the stage they went . . . time after time, playing to less than receptive crowds. The practiced smile of the actor's mask was all that covered the heartbreak inside. The sound of laughter that had kept them going all those years was all but gone.

Toward the End of the Journey, the True Rewards Are Revealed

Behind the scenes, and unknown to Moe, Columbia planned on re-releasing a series of old Stooges shorts — many dating back to the 1930s — through their newly formed TV subsidiary Screen Gems. The package held little hope of success and was being offered at a bargain price.

The series hit television, and within one week, the shorts became the number one television series in the nation. The Stooges were bringing the gift of laughter to the world once again, but this time, they were playing to a new audience — children.

For the first time in their career, they were actually making money. In one week's time, they went from earning $2,500 for a six-day week, to $25,000 for a one-day dedication of a shopping mall in New York. They played to packed houses all over the country.

In 1971, the Stooges began work on a new feature film, *Kook's Tour*, costarring Moose, a black Labrador retriever. During a short break in production, just days before the final filming, Larry suffered a paralyzing, career-ending stroke.

Moe arranged for Larry to be taken to the Motion Picture Country Home Hospital in Woodland Hills, California, where he would be able to receive the care he needed, and at no cost to him.

Moe visited Larry faithfully every weekend. Moe would push Larry's wheelchair around while he played shuffleboard with the other patients. On his visits, Moe would always find Larry telling jokes to the other patients in an attempt to lift their spirits.

During the years Larry spent in the hospital, Moe kept busy touring the country. He did some guest appearances and worked the local talk-show circuit, keeping the Stooges' purpose alive. Moe knew God created laughter to ease the pain of human suffering and to shed light in a sea of darkness. The Stooges' most-cherished compensation for a lifelong work was the sweet song of laughter.

On the morning of January 24, 1975, the telephone rang. It was Larry's daughter calling. Larry had died. Moe's heart was once again broken. The two old friends had shared so much together. They had spent a lifetime bringing laughter and joy to millions and getting so much in return. Less than four months later, on May 4, Moe succumbed to the lung cancer that had been ravaging his body for over two years — drawing the final curtain on a legacy that would outlast a lifetime.

I am confident that you will recognize your own personal servant vision when it appears to you, and it is my hope that I have inspired you to prepare yourself to take the steps necessary to follow it wherever it leads you. May you be granted, by the powers of the universe, the courage and resolve to walk your path to its very end.

CHAPTER 16

Act with Faith

Much of what we do and how we act as servant leaders seems to be counterintuitive. To others, it may look dead wrong. Such is the case with the suggestion there is no need to follow a prescribed plan. We have all been conditioned to have a plan of action in place before we take any kind of action on our own. Although this is good advice for more worldly things, it is possibly the greatest cause of failure in a servant leader's ability to see his or her vision through. I can only articulate it this way and hope you'll understand: A plan is like a map. It tells you where to go when the road ahead becomes unfamiliar. When you are traveling with a guide who lives on the road ahead, you don't need a map. So, in following your servant vision, abandon your notion of a concrete plan of action and your need to have one in place before you set off. Trust that you are being guided to do something that is most likely bigger than your ability to even imagine. I liken it to being a piece in a cosmic jigsaw puzzle. We take our rightful place so that others can fit together with us, and together we make up something bigger than any one of us can see.

Following Your Servant Vision

Following your servant vision does not require you to take a leap of faith as much as it requires a *walk of faith*, placing one foot in front of the other, one confidently uncertain step at a time. The following pointers should assist you:

Take action, even without a plan. When you are walking with the guide, you don't need a map. Simply focus on your vision and begin walking with the faith that everything you will need will be there for you when you need it. There will be tests, obstacles, and setbacks ahead. You will be walking blindly into dark and unfamiliar territory, so it is important to know that the one who led you to this point will also be the one to see you through.

Your faith, talents, abilities, relationships, and resources will be tested. The evil in the world does not want to see good triumph. Your faith will protect you from harm and will carry you over the obstacles.

Trust you will have what you need. Everything you need to succeed will be there when you need it, although it usually shows up according to a time frame that may not be your own.

Maintain your tenacity and faith. There will be tests along the way, times when nothing seems to be going your way, when every indication says "Quit, you fool!" At such times, you must vow not to quit, no matter what.

Remember, people you trust the most may present the strongest opposition to your pursuit. Only you can see your vision; it was given to you alone.

God made you uniquely qualified to help him attain his goal. This is the point where your relationship with God becomes essential. You can trust that it will all work out as long as you hold onto his hand and walk with him. The spirit in which you proceed is also important: you must do what you are doing, not to please God, but to thank God for choosing you to become part of his divine plan.

Sometimes the investment you are called to make is very high, both for you and for those you love. I had to give up my business activities and spent tens of thousands of dollars, often when I could least afford to do so in order to follow my servant vision. This resulted in many hardships for me and my family. But remember this, just when it looks like you can't take it any longer, the clouds will break and a beam of the brightest sunlight you have ever seen will touch your face, and then you will know that you are doing what you were called to do.

There will come times when things seem to come to a screeching halt for no apparent reason. Most likely, the reason is something you can't even see. I refer to these periods of no progress as "transition periods." When these periods occur, I remain patient and understand that I am being held back for a reason. But I didn't always understand.

Understanding Transition Periods

I was speaking at a convention in Baltimore, Maryland, in early fall. The hotels in the city were booked solid, so I had to stay twenty minutes out of town. Rather than drive and fight for a parking space, I took the advice of a friend and rode the light-rail into the city.

All went well on my trip into the city; the problems came on the way back to my hotel. Although it was unseasonably warm that day, a cold front made its way through the area and on its heels came a band of torrential thunderstorms. As fate would have it, I was completely unprepared, lacking both raincoat and umbrella. By the time I finally settled onto the train, I was soaking wet, cold, and tired. I was not looking forward to my 5 A.M. wake-up call. All I wanted to do was get back to my hotel, change out of my soaked clothes, and get some sleep.

The end of the third day, in a ten-day-long trip, had not yet drawn to a close and already I was feeling completely enervated. I looked down at the suit I was wearing, which represented half of my traveling wardrobe. A feeling of disgust took hold. My favorite suit was filled with permanent wrinkles, stained with mud, and smelled like an old, damp horse blanket. I sunk deep into my seat, dreading the week ahead, and gazed at the visions of self-pity that played on the movie screen of the darkened tramcar windows. I was feeling pretty low.

About fifteen minutes into the trip, the bottom dropped out. Without warning, the train car filled with a deafening shrieking sound. Wheels screeching, the train began to buck and weave, then it slammed unexpectedly to a halt. I was tossed onto the floor like a damp rag doll. I lay in a crumpled pile on the train floor for a moment and just listened. The train sat dead quiet. Not a sound could be heard except for the quiet hum of the motor. I picked myself up off the floor, crawled back into my seat, and just sat for a moment, trying to figure out what had just happened.

This is how we often feel when an unexpected setback knocks us off our feet. Crises and setbacks come at us almost exclusively without warning and, for some reason, seem to come when we can least afford them. As if sent to knock us down, grab our attention, and hold it for a moment, a volley of crises and setbacks leaves very little emotion in us, except numbness — and soon the numbness gives way to anger.

I sat in the empty train car, unable to see out of the darkened windows. The black of night gave no indication of what had gone wrong. I became angry: I wanted to know what was causing the train to sit still on the tracks, preventing me from reaching my destination and the warm bed that beckoned my cold, tired, now-aching body. I stared at the tear in my pants. I grew increasingly anxious as the minutes passed. My lack of control over the situation, coupled with no information as to the cause of our abrupt stop and ensuing delay, resulted in great personal angst. To put it plainly, *I was getting really pissed off.*

Dealing with the Negatives

We often confront these same feelings of anxiety, tension, fear, disappointment, anger, resentment, and denial when crisis rears its ugly head and obstacles spring up to block our path. We are moving effortlessly along our path, our goal well within sight, and, without warning, we are blindsided by problems, setbacks, and seemingly insurmountable obstacles. It is a natural, human predisposition to feel anxious and angry at times like these. We are drawn into these feelings by both lack of knowledge about the reason for our dilemma and our own selfish nature. The hardest thing to do at this time is to step outside our selfish needs and desires and try to find meaning in the events that have interrupted our plans. But this is exactly what we must do if we are to attach meaning to these troublesome events and forestall the natural temptation to give up when times get tough.

After what seemed to be a lifetime, but was actually more like five minutes, the train conductor emerged from the forward compartment with word of what had happened. The storm had caused a huge tree to fall and block the tracks. A quick reaction on the part of the train operator prevented a disaster. The discomfort and inconvenience I was in the process of lamenting paled in comparison to what might have been had the train collided with that hundred-year-old oak tree at sixty miles per hour. New knowledge brought with it a whole new set of feelings, with relief leading the pack.

I once viewed setbacks and transition periods with resentment and self-pity. These are common human reactions to what we might perceive to be negative events in our lives. And, as the saying goes, old habits die hard. I still momentarily slip into the blind self-pity trap, mildly succumbing to the same old feelings and misconceptions about the circumstances that have thrust themselves on me...and so will you.

Making the Most of Setbacks

I think you remember my friend Bill, the businessman who found himself a million dollars in debt and then made a fortune by collecting bad debts. When he founded Commercial Financial Services (CFS), Bill set out to revolutionize the debt-collection business by simply treating people with dignity and respect, and history shows he did it. During the six-year period from the 1991 to 1997, CFS grew from a fledgling company employing twenty people and earning just over $141,000, to an industry giant (dominating over 52 percent of the U.S. debt market) employing over four thousand people and netting more than $187 million. I guess you might say doing the right thing really pays off. By 1997, my friend Bill was reaping the rewards of service and enjoying the recognition he most certainly deserved. I'd be hard-pressed to enumerate all of the business and community-service awards my friend received during his tenure as head of CFS, but I'd venture to say that his most treasured are the ones that honor his commitment to the betterment of people, both customers and employees, and recognition of his personal honesty and sense of fair play.

A servant leader's actions attract many riches and personal rewards, this is true; but his actions can also attract jealousy and animus. Where there is good being done, there will always be evil trying to stop it. I told this to Bill one afternoon not long ago as a way of trying to make sense out of a senseless attack that had been leveled against CFS and Bill personally.

In 1998, an anonymous letter was sent to the United States Securities and Exchange Commission alleging CFS and Bill of wrongdoing. The governmental regulators responded to the allegations with predictable blind zealousness, hiring an army of special investigators and auditors and conducting closed-door meetings with CFS's bankers and investors. The result was just as predictable: panic.

It did not matter that the allegations were later proven to be spurious and both Bill and his company were found to be totally without fault; the damage was done, and the once profitable CFS was left in a shambles.

During our conversation, Bill confided his feelings to me, and, in his words, I could see the mark of a true servant leader: "I've been a piñata for the financial industry for a year and a half, but that doesn't bother me. What bothers me the most," Bill said, "is what is going to happen to the employees and customers of CFS — both are going to be left worse off because of the evil that was aimed at me."

I reminded Bill of the role of a servant leader: to spit in the face of evil and use his personal pain to sharpen his skills and fortify his will to serve. "Go out and find something that only you can do," I told him. "Get back on your horse and ride."

It's hard for us to see past our own problems and focus on serving others, especially when we are up to our necks in trouble and grief. But, for a seasoned servant leader like Bill, it often takes only a reminder.

A few months later, I got a package in the mail. It was from Bill. Inside the envelope was a business plan for a new venture and a little yellow Post-it note that read: "So, what do you think?"

In *A Farewell to Arms*, Ernest Hemingway wrote: "The world breaks everyone and afterward many are strong at the broken places." I'm not certain, but I think Hemingway had a servant leader in mind when he wrote those words. My friend Bill was back — and in a big way. His new business venture, Neighborhood Financial Centers, is poised to serve a huge segment of society: the 45 percent of Americans whose income is less than $25,000 per year and who don't have a relationship with a "legitimate" financial institution.

Neighborhood Financial Centers is as unique as my friend Bill. Imagine a shopping-mall-style building (complete with a food court and supervised play area for children) devoted entirely to serving the financial needs of the low-income communities throughout the nation. According to Bill's plan, the freestanding centers will offer such services as "loan shark free" signature loans at reasonable interest rates, credit counseling services, money management classes, low-cost legal services, health and accident insurance, checking and savings accounts, tax return preparation, utility payments, and phone service restoration, just to name a few. Plus the centers will reserve rent-free space for local social service agencies. This new social approach to financial services is etched by the mark of the servant leader's universal goal — to leave those you serve stronger, more independent, and better able to serve the needs of others.

Nothing Lasts Forever

I don't think any of us can sit watching our whole world turn to rubble and think, "Oh goodie! Another transition period!" If we did, we might be ready for that padded room everyone keeps talking about.

It is normal to feel anger, frustration, and anxiety at times like these, at least for a moment or two. The important thing is to get past these feelings as quickly as possible. We need to hop off the self-pity train and learn from the lessons of life. Armed with new knowledge and insight, we can step off onto solid ground and continue walking toward our goals.

Nature shows us that there is no condition that is permanent. As the tide ebbs, so it surely flows; as Longfellow wrote, "the lowest ebb it is when the tide turns."

I have been through a number of monumental transition periods in my life, as have you. It's not fun going into them, but I'm sure you'll agree, it feels great coming out! The light of experience has helped me to look at the crises and setbacks that mark the beginning of all transition periods in a different way. I now view them simply as a signal that the universe is at work around me and that my life is about to change in a significant way. The object here is to not just *go* through these experiences but to *grow* through them.

What to Do When You Find Yourself Entering a Transition Period

Looking at my own life and the lives of many servant leaders, there is no set time frame for how long these transition periods will last. Some last only a brief while (like the train delay in Baltimore) and others take years. The process for *growing* through them is the same in both:

1. Get excited! Okay, at least try. Understand that you will emerge from this experience a better, stronger person, capable of far more than you were when you first entered the period.

2. Stay positive. Increase your journaling. Write, in great detail, about your experiences, thoughts, and feelings. My friend Tracy Clark keeps what she calls her "grateful journal" during times of transition. In it, she lists

things that she is grateful for each day: "I'm grateful for being blessed with talent to sing, for being in good health, for not having another flat tire on my way to the audition." She told me that this practice has helped her stay positive and focused on what matters most during some of the hardest periods of her life.

3. Keep in close touch with the universe. Meditate, pray, take time to be quiet. Listen for guidance. Increase the time you spend alone doing nothing but listening for guidance.

4. Keep a watch out for other visionary leaders to appear bringing with them messages and help. They may come in any guise — people you know, people you have never met, in the form of the written word, even in recordings. Stay in tune with the universe, knowing that help is on the way.

5. Stay in motion. Action wards off the negativity, anxiety, and depression that can accompany these periods. Continue doing what you were doing before the period began, until a message comes telling you either to go in a different direction or resume your forward trek. If the events of the period prevent you from physically doing what you did before, do something else — anything! The important thing is to avoid sitting and doing nothing but feeling sorry for yourself. Occupy your time with things that do not require "thinking." Do something physical like gardening, or take a long, brisk walk.

6. Keep your WHY in focus. Keep a memento of your servant vision in front of you at all times, carry it with you, keep it on your desk at work and on the nightstand at night.

7. Stay in touch with your network. Your visionary leaders

network can lend you the support you need to overcome the obstacles in your path. The powers of this mastermind alliance can help you in many ways, but only if you are open to the help. Call the people who are supportive of your vision and talk to them; they can, if nothing else, understand the frustration you are going through.

8. Stop trying to control the outcome. Experience the transition period as a piece of clay in the potter's hands. The clay does not resist the potter; it remains malleable and yields to the wishes of the potter. Allow yourself to be molded by the universe without regard to manner or shape. Trust in the universe's plan.

9. Avoid the natural tendency to focus on the crisis itself and the negativity that looms over as a result. Look for the opportunity that is inherent in all crises, and when you find it, lock onto it and don't let go.

Mixing up a Miracle

You just never know what you'll become part of when you take up your servant vision. It was late June, 1936. The sun hung high amid the puffy white clouds that adorned the crisp blue, midday sky. A calm breeze blew, rustling the leaves of an old elm tree that stood beside a small, faded gray house at the end of a quiet cul-de-sac in the northeast end of Pittsburgh.

It was a picture-perfect day. The neighborhood children were busy playing hide-and-seek, scampering through the yards and hiding among the shrubbery. A stout woman dressed in a red-and-white polka-dot dress and white linen apron tended her rose garden. The rhythmic whir of a push mower could be heard off in the distance. Everyone seemed to be outside enjoying this beautiful summer day; everyone, that is, except Frederick Osius.

Frederick Osius sat tinkering with his latest invention,

completely unaware of the beautiful day that nature had created just outside his gloomy basement workshop window. His latest invention, dubbed "a disintegrating mixer for producing fluent substances," was having some problems. It seemed as if the seal that was supposed to keep the liquid within the tall glass container was not designed properly. Osius watched as a liquidy mess oozed through the seal and onto the counter. The silly thing just did not work, in spite of five years of personal effort and $25,000 of his, his relatives', and his friends' money.

Osius had another problem. Not only had he run out of money, but now it seemed as if every time he walked down the street, people ducked inside their houses. No doubt they were attempting to avoid his constant requests for deeper investment.

Osius heard a story about the famous bandleader Fred Waring. Prior to becoming a leader of his big band, Fred Waring and the Pennsylvanians, Waring attended the University of Pennsylvania School of Engineering and was himself an admitted gadgeteer. Osius knew that Waring was making it big in the big band business, so with his present funding stream reduced to a drip, Osius figured he might as well hit up the famous and wealthy bandleader for some cash.

Legend has it that Osius found out through a friend that the Pennsylvanians would be playing at the famous Vanderbilt Theater in New York City on a certain Saturday night. So, our hero, gadget in hand, hopped the next train bound for the Great White Way.

Pursuing Your Servant Vision Draws Others to Your Aid

In addition to his inventing prowess, Osius was known to possess a sterling tongue. Once in New York, he negotiated his way backstage and into the entertainer's dressing room without a hitch. Osius was prepared. He had taken the time to learn intimate details about the famous bandleader. He had discovered that Waring had a fondness for bananas. Once inside Waring's dressing room, Osius, while pitching the merits of his contraption, produced a stalk of the tropical delicacy and a pint of fresh cold milk. Ingredients at the ready, he began immediately whipping up a velvety banana milk shake, which he presented, to the delight of the bandleader.

That must have been some sales talk given by our eccentric young hero, clad in his trademark striped pants and a bright lemon-yellow tie and holding a fistful of banana mush. Waring bought! With the bandleader's money, the two went on to patent and produce the first Waring Disintegrating Blendor, with an *o*.

With the help of Waring's engineer friend Ed Lee, who fixed the leaks, and German designer Peter Muller-Munk, who gave the Blendor its famous polished, art deco look of chrome and glass, the Miracle Mixer, as it was called at the time, made its debut at the National Restaurant Show in Chicago in 1937. It was an instant hit.

Sales of the Blendor continued briskly until the Japanese put a halt to its production on December 7, 1941, when the first bomb fell on Pearl Harbor. The war creamed the Blendor market. Sales plummeted to sure bankruptcy levels, and it looked as if the Blendor had whipped its last banana when, entering into the picture was an angel, or another visionary leader, by the name of Hazard Reeves.

Just When You Think It's Over . . .

Reeves, a professional salesman, saw promise in the future of the Blendor, so much so that he bought the company. Why keep the Blendor only in restaurants? Reeves questioned. He opened up the home market, and sales skyrocketed: the one-millionth Waring Blendor sold in 1954.

The Paths of Servant Leaders Always Intersect

No doubt the result of a creative inspiration, Reeves changed the design of the Blendor, making it applicable for hospital use. One of the first newly named Waring Aseptical Dispersal Blendors was purchased by the hospital at Harvard University, where another team of servant leaders led by John Elders was working on culturing the polio virus.

It was here that two different groups of people, each with unique talents and skills, each pursuing distinctly different visions, collided. The New Aseptical Blendor sped production of the culture medium, allowing another servant leader, Dr. Jonas Edward Salk, to develop a vaccine that was used to conquer the dreaded childhood killer known as polio.

One last bit of advice: Expect to be rewarded. Many rewards will come to you as you progress along the way toward the fulfillment of your servant vision. You will begin to notice an interesting thing about these rewards: the rewards will likely come to you in manner and form unlike those you would have been capable of generating yourself. They come in such a way, and with such intensity, that there will be no doubt they have been given to you by God. In these rewards, you will often find the things that bring you the most joy and pleasure. Think about it: you never would have known them if you had decided not to take this journey or had given into your desire to quit.

A Servant Leader's Mission Lives on Forever

After years on stage and screen, and changes of cast because of tragic losses, the saga of the Three Stooges might have ended when Moe, the original and last Stooge, died on May 4, 1975. The light of a servant leader is not so easily extinguished, however, and the saga of the Three Stooges did not end there. Only recently, after speaking to a small group of servant leaders working in the biomedical field, I made my way through the hospital corridors toward my car. As I passed the pediatric oncology unit, the sound of hysterical laughter caught my attention. I poked my head in to see where it was coming from. There, seated in a corner of the room, was a group of young children, all of whom were obviously patients undergoing painful and debilitating rounds of chemotherapy. They were all huddled around a television set, laughing uncontrollably. I walked in closer to see what was so funny, and there on the screen was a scene from an old black-and-white Stooges' short. The servant leaders may be gone, but their mission lives on.

What miracles are you destined to become a part of? Will you become a willing participant or an astonished bystander? The choices you make in your life will most certainly determine your destiny. Choose to become a servant leader, and you just might change the course of history.

Your first act of servant leadership should be one of giving. The greatest gifts we can give another are encouragement and enlightenment. To this end, my suggestion is simple: Purchase another copy of this book and give it to a total stranger. Just imagine what kind of world we can create together if each of us inspires just one other person to become a servant leader.

I also encourage you to give the gift of inspiration in the form of your own personal story. Please write or E-mail me with your experiences as you work to place your unique mark on the face of time. Who knows, you just might see your story in an upcoming book.

Alexander J. Berardi
Box 1283
Wall Township, New Jersey 07719-1283
E-mail: Mail@AlexanderBerardi.com

Books by Other Servant Leaders

Frankl, Viktor. *Man's Search for Meaning: An Introduction to Logotherapy*. Boston: Beacon Press, 1959. Originally published in Germany in 1946 under the title *Ein Psycholog erlebt das Konzentrationslager*.

Greenleaf, Robert K. *On Becoming a Servant Leader*. San Francisco: Jossey-Bass, 1996.

———. *Servant Leadership: A Journey into the Nature of Legitimate Power and Greatness*. New York: Paulist Press, 1977.

Jaworski, Joseph. *Synchronicity: The Inner Path of Leadership*. San Francisco: Berrett-Koehler, 1996.

Teresa, Mother. *No Greater Love*. Novato, Calif.: New World Library, 1997.

Ziglar, Zig. *See You at the Top*. 25th anniversary rev. ed. Gretna, La.: Pelican Publishing, 2000.

———. *Staying Up, Up, Up in a Down, Down World*. Nashville, Tenn.: Thomas Nelson, 2000.

On the Science of Selfishness

Dawkins, Richard. *The Selfish Gene.* New York: Oxford University Press, 1976.

On Spirituality

Abadie, M. J. *Awaken to Your Spiritual Self.* Holbrook, Mass.: Adams Media Corporation, 1998.

Blackaby, Henry T., and Claude V. King. *Experiencing God: How to Live the Full Adventure of Knowing and Doing the Will of God.* Nashville, Tenn.: Broadman & Holman Publishers, 1994.

Carlson, Richard, and Benjamin Shield. *For the Love of God: Handbook for the Spirit.* Novato, Calif.: New World Library, 1997.

Hopkins, Jasper. *Nicholas of Cusa on Learned Ignorance: A Translation and an Appraisal of* De Docta Ignorantia. Minneapolis: The Arthur J. Banning Press, 1985.

May, Rollo. *Man's Search for Himself.* New York: W. W. Norton & Company, 1953.

On Managing Change

Ritsema, Rudolph, and Stephen Karcher. *I Ching: The Classic Chinese Oracle of Change: The First Complete Translation with Concordance.* New York: Barnes & Noble, 1995.

On Developing Heightened Awareness

Dalai Lama. *Ethics for the New Millennium.* New York: Riverhead Books, 1999.

Hall, Doug. *Jump Start Your Brain.* New York: Warner Books, 1995.

Kilham, Christopher. *The Five Tibetans: Five Dynamic Exercises for Health, Energy, and Personal Power.* Rochester, Vt.: Healing Arts Press, 1994.

Progoff, Ira. *At a Journal Workshop: Writing to Access the Power of the Unconscious and Evoke Creative Ability.* New York: Tarcher, 1992.

Wilson, Paul. *The Calm Technique: Meditation without Magic or Mysticism.* New York: Barnes & Noble, 1999.

On Personal Finance

Burkett, Larry. *Debt-Free Living: How to Get Out of Debt and Stay Out.* New York: Moody Press, 2000.

Kiyosaki, Robert T., and Sharon L. Lechter. *Rich Dad, Poor Dad: What the Rich Teach Their Kids about Money That the Poor and Middle Class Do Not!* New York: Warner Books, 1997.

Ramsey, Karen. *Everything You Know about Money Is Wrong: Overcome the Financial Myths Keeping You from the Life You Want.* New York: Regan Books, 1999.

Savage, Terry. *The Savage Truth on Money.* New York: John Wiley & Sons, 1999.

Index

About the Author

Alexander J. Berardi serves as chairman emeritus of the Alexander Group, which owns and manages a variety of service and retail businesses. These businesses, through the talents of hundreds of exceptional servant leaders, serve the evolving needs of a diverse society. As an example of his own message, he left his business interests behind so he might help others to discover and use their hidden talents and lead their own revolutionary organizations into the future.

As a leadership strategist, he helps others to internalize the principles of servant leadership and develop organizations that are poised to take full advantage of the future. He addresses business and trade association audiences of all sizes. Using his unique combination of humor and personal stories, he inspires and challenges listeners to pursue their talents and vision. These future servant leaders will discover cures for diseases that will plague us in the future, invent solutions to problems still unknown, and become market leaders in yet undiscovered fields. Through his writings, he shows readers how to — no matter what their chosen field or level of comfort — tap into and use the hidden greatness that lies waiting in us all. He shares his life with his wife Diane between the New Jersey Coast and the Blue Ridge Mountains.

New World Library is dedicated to publishing
books, audiocassettes, and videotapes that
inspire and challenge us to improve the quality
of our lives and our world.

Our books and tapes are available
in bookstores everywhere.
For a catalog of our complete library
of fine books and cassettes, contact:

New World Library
14 Pamaron Way
Novato, CA 94949

Phone: (415) 884-2100
Fax: (415) 884-2199
Or call toll-free (800) 972-6657
Catalog requests: Ext. 50
Ordering: Ext. 52

E-mail: escort@nwlib.com
www.newworldlibrary.com